BANDIT'S GREAT ESCAPE

RACHEL RIVERS PORTER

Illustrated by MATTHEW and ROSIE JACKSON

Bandit's Great Escape

Illustrations by Rosie Jackson
Cover by Matthew Jackson

First published 2024

Rivers Porter Publishing, Great Britain
Imprint ref: 240607a
riversporter.com

Paperback
ISBN: 978-0-9956570-4-5

Praise from Children for
Bandit's Great Escape

'I was extremely engaged and pulled into the story incredibly quickly. I couldn't stop reading, it was sooooo good!'
Reader's Favourite, child reader feedback:
WriteMentor Novel-in-Development Award 2023.

'I loved the book and I'd recommend it to everyone in my class. I really liked the characters especially Bandit, Isla and Rat, and I enjoyed laughing at the two bumbling crooks.'
Raphael 10

'I really liked how Croaky is trying to make Bandit into a human by teaching him to sit at the table to eat. She was lonely and stressed as she had issues, and he made her happy.'
Ruth 10

'I loved reading Bandit's Great Escape. I particularly liked how Bandit made good friends with Nero the rottweiler, and how they both changed as characters.'
Joshua 12

'It's one of the best books I've ever read. Bandit's Great Escape is 2nd in my Top Ten books after Mary Poppins and equal with Black Beauty.'
Hannah 8

'I really enjoyed how Bandit kept changing from playful when Croaky taught him to have manners, then he changed back to a normal dog. I liked Rat's personality - he was trying to help Bandit escape, but also trying to help himself by getting food off Bandit!'
Holly 10

'*This is the best dog adventure I've ever read. Wonderfully written, it is exciting, captivating and full of heart.*'

Philip Kavvadias, author of *Mission Microraptor*

'*Bandit is a great character, with a fabulous voice and personality - he has so much to endure, but never really loses his joy.*'

Emma Read, author of *Milton the Mighty*

In Memory of

My beautiful dog Jessie, whose faithfulness, fun and friendship was the inspiration for the character of Bandit. You are greatly missed and I will always love you.

And Malcolm Cave, one of the kindest people I've known, who could always walk my dog to heel - whereas it looked like Jessie was taking me for a walk!

Drawing of Jessie by Peter Thurman

https://www.youtube.com/@ThurmanArt
Drawing a Golden Retriever in Pencil and Charcoal

1. Running Like the Wind

Another case came downstairs with a bump, bump, bump, shaking the floorboards. I looked up at Mum and whined. The hall had been filling up all morning, but I felt empty, like something was being taken away. I wanted to curl up and hide in my basket, but it was propped against the row of tall cases. They smelt musty, unfamiliar. I arched my neck to see over the barrier.

Where were the shoes and socks that usually littered the floor? My lead was still hanging on the coat stand, but the jackets were piled by the door and Mum's squishy bag with the long straps was lying on top.

Something was gnawing at my insides, digging a hole, so it wasn't my fault that I leapt up and attacked the bag. When something's soft, it's an invitation to chew. I shook my head from side to side; if I tore bits off, the worry might disappear.

"Get off my handbag!"

I froze, the bag swaying in my mouth. Mum

sounded cross and she was scrunching her hair in her fingers. Maybe she's got fleas? My ears flattened and I backed away, tail between my legs.

"Stop getting at Bandit, it's not *his* fault." When Isla rushed in from the kitchen, the tip of my tail swished the floor. She sat on the stairs and stroked my silky ears, strands of her hair tickling my whiskers. "Why can't Bandit come with us?"

"You know why."

I lifted a paw asking to sit on Isla's lap, then she unfolded her arms and crushed her head against my fur. Waves of sadness washed into me and I snuggled closer. **I'm here for you, we're in this together.**

Mum's shout broke us apart.

"What now?" Isla's voice rippled my ears. As her knees moved, I jumped down and followed. Mum was kneeling on a large bag, tugging the zip. The bag didn't like it as it was squeaking.

Isla leant over to help. "Can I take Bandit down the beach?"

"Sorry, there's no time."

"But he's shaking. You can't do this — he'll try and find us and we'll be a million miles away."

"Stop exaggerating, Isla, you're getting over-excitable like Bandit."

"I *want* to be like Bandit, at least he *cares* about me!" The pain in Isla's voice made me whimper.

Mum stared at me. "Just get that dog out of here, please."

"So I *can* take Bandit for a walk?" said Isla.

WALK! I jumped up and chased my tail.

Why was Mum laughing now? I've never understood human laughter. Sometimes it races around the room and catches people like it's alive, and sometimes it vanishes.

Isla's lips lifted, but her eyes weren't smiling. "Bandit wants to stay with us — look, he's wagging his tail."

"Bandit likes me best," said Harry, bouncing into the hall. "He's wagging his whole bottom now." He rushed towards me, dipping his arms from side to side. "We're going on an aeroplane. *Woohoo*!"

Not this again. Isla's brother may be little for a human, but he's still heavy when he sits on you; and it's not fun when your ears are used as aeroplane wings.

The zip screeched, then Mum let go. "Go on then.

But don't let Bandit in the sea, his fur's a nightmare to dry when it's matted."

Isla leapt up. "Thanks!"

"No more than twenty minutes and don't be late."

A whoosh of joy flooded into me — Isla's eyes were glowing with that special look. She whistled and flapped my bandana. **Our Secret Code.** My legs tingled and excitement fizzed down to my tail. I stretched my front paws and bowed, then she tied the bandana around my neck. **Come on!** I bounced around the coat stand while Isla unhooked my lead. I raced to the door, then she pushed the top half open and the smell of the sea rushed in.

We headed along the coast path. Waves were crashing on the beach and exciting messages were flying in the wind. I'm a secret agent and every tuft of grass has to be investigated. Every mossy wall. Every molehill. You find out all these things when you sniff. **A whole world is waiting out there and all you have to do is to use your nose.** Humans just look with their eyes and walk straight past, but I always know when someone's been here before us. Like the sheepdog with the yummy odour from the farm, the type you want to rub all over. I don't know why humans have this thing against cow muck, rolling in it is the best fun.

Once we climbed down the cliff path, Isla crouched down and cuddled me. Then she reached into her pocket and held her phone high above us. "Look at the camera, Bandit!" There was a bright flash in my eyes.

I was glad when Isla let me off the lead. I darted across the pebbles to investigate trails along the bumpy worm casts and scents hidden in strings of seaweed.

What's that? Ooo, smells nice! This is the best time: seeing which friends have been here, then covering their scent with my pee — showing I know who they are, and letting them know I've been here too.

Isla's voice pulled me back. She was sitting on a rock, hugging her knees. I bounded over and nosed under her arm. The wind was flicking her hair across her cheeks but she stared straight ahead. My eyes never left her face, but she didn't throw a ball for me and we didn't splash into the sea. We just sat.

I licked her cheek and it tasted salty. Her lips wobbled. "I'll miss you so much, Bandit, you're my best friend." Her eyes started to leak. "Dad said he's going to make lots of money in Dubai so builders can work on our cottage." She rubbed the back of her hand over her nose. "I don't care if there's a hole in the roof; why can't we stay here forever?"

She suddenly sprang up. "Come on!" We ran, my long ears flapping and her hair splashing around her face. We chased across the sand faster than birds, then lay down and faced the sky. It was wild like us. We were one: the girl who ran like the wind, and me.

I moved first because I sniffed Mum's scent drifting in the breeze. Then I heard a ringing sound. Isla pulled out her phone.

"Yes, but… Please Mum, just another five minutes?" Isla thrust her phone in her pocket, then we nosed along the beach, my snout and her hands side by side — a tasty tissue for me, and a shell for her.

A cry reached us and Isla arched her neck and did that thing humans sometimes do: pressing a hand against their eyebrows. I picked up a stone in my teeth and dropped it at Isla's feet, willing her to play, but her eyes didn't sparkle like they usually did. She sighed. "Time to go."

I tugged her hand. **What's wrong? Why can't we stay here and play?**

2. Secrets

When we reached the cottage, fear nibbled at my throat. I curled into a ball on the mat watching Dad lift cases into the car boot.

He closed it, then turned to Isla. "Good walk?"

WALK! I leapt up and wagged my tail, but Isla shook her head. "You've already been on one." My tail fell because Isla sounded sad. Her eyes began to leak again. "We can't leave Bandit, it's not fair." The pain in Isla's voice made me whine. I nosed her hand so her fingers uncurled, then she wrapped her arms around me. "I love you so much, Bandit."

I snuggled closer and closed my eyes. **This is my best place, my happy place, just me and Isla.**

But Dad said something and we had to move. I brushed against Isla's legs as she followed him into the house and joined the rest of our family.

Mum leant down to stroke me. "Don't worry Bandit. Mrs Mandeville's looking forward to having you. She lives on her own, she lost her husband many years ago."

"Where?" said Harry.

Isla tutted and rolled her eyes. Humans do all these weird expressions. They also talk with their hands like Mum was doing, wagging her finger. "That's enough Isla. You're five years older than Harry; you can't expect a seven-year-old to know that." There was a jingle as she touched her wrist. "Everyone been to the toilet? Traffic's very busy in July and we've got an hour's detour across Bodmin Moor to drop off Bandit."

I heard my name and gazed at Mum. She rattled some keys. "Grandad said he might come over to check on the cottage and take out the bins, but…"

"Grandad *never* comes here," said Isla.

Silence. Tension was swirling around. Mum raised her eyebrows at Dad and his eyelids narrowed. **What was happening?**

"Why doesn't anyone ever tell me anything?" said Isla. More secret messages flew between Mum and Dad, then Mum herded the children outside.

Dad sucked a bulging plastic bag out of the bin and propped it by the door, then he sank onto the stairs. I caught a whiff of last night's fish and chips merging with his usual nutty smell of paint, but the hole inside me was so deep, I wasn't hungry. I rested my chin on his knees and he laid his hand on my back.

"You know something's up, don't you, Boy? It's such a mess. I didn't want to come back to live here after everything that happened..." His breath shuddered and I sensed pain deep inside, like he was far away even though he was here. "But now I don't want to leave."

I love car journeys — the whizz of speed, the buzz of excitement — but this time I panted in anxiety. Something felt wrong. Isla was sighing and twisting my bandana around her fingers.

Why has it come off? Aren't we going to the long beach where you can run and run?

We stopped outside a large stone house. Each window had smaller windows inside it like eyes watching me. The car boot banged, and Dad walked towards the house, through a gate and up a path that crunched underfoot. He was carrying my basket. I could smell dog biscuits inside it and my food and water bowls.

I shrank closer to Isla and her breathing went all

jagged as we got out of the car. The door to the house opened and a woman, hunched over a long stick, creaked her neck to look up at Dad.

A sticky smell of rotting fish hung around her. She was shorter than Isla, and almost as round as she was high, but when she opened her mouth, it was so wide that it touched the edge of her cheeks.

"Hello, Joey. So this is your pup…" She leant towards me. "We're going to have so much fun, aren't we, my beauty?

Isla's hand tightened on my collar and I pressed closer to her.

The woman looked at Dad again. "I hope you'll stay for a cuppa and a bite to eat?" Her eyes glowed behind large round glasses. "You always loved my baking, didn't you?"

Dad looked at his shoes. "Sorry I haven't been over recently."

"Three years ago. Christmas Eve." The stick jabbed the ground, making me flinch. I like sticks when people throw them, just not smacking near my nose. I watched the woman's expression, wary of any sharp movements as she kept talking. "I made chocolate chip cookies and

16

you gave me a chocolate orange."

"Is it that long?" Dad wriggled his shoulders like he had an itch he couldn't scratch. Everyone seemed to have fleas today.

The woman nodded. Her glasses nodded, too, and nearly fell off. Harry giggled. "Can *I* have a chocolate orange?"

"Not now," said Mum. She looked at the woman in the doorway. "We're so grateful that you're looking after Bandit." She glanced at Dad. "Aren't we, Joe?"

His feet shuffled like he was squishing a crumb. He

bent to attach my lead. "Sorry, we don't have much time…"

The fishy-smelling woman with the wobbly glasses said, "I see." Her mouth shrank at the edges, drooping either side of her chin. Then her long skirt swished. "Let's have him then."

Isla tried to hold onto me, but the stick stabbed the lead, trapping me. I edged away from the woman's sandals and bare feet. I like cheese if I find grated bits on the floor, just not between toes.

Dad lifted my basket and the food inside. "It's only a year, Bandit," he said in a trembling voice, "then we'll be back for you, I promise."

The woman grasped my collar. "He can have your old room, Joey." She yanked the lead and pulled me inside.

"Wait," Isla cried, "Bandit needs this!" She ran to the woman, pressing my bandana into her wrinkled hand.

The door banged. They were gone.

3. The Croaky Stranger

Silence except for the croaky breath and the stick tap-tapping. No happy bouncing children, no laughter, just the old woman and me. I nosed my bandana, sniffing every part of it. I could smell traces of food and salty seaweed and sand. And the girl who ran like the wind. Nothing in the world was like Isla's sweet scent. I lay down with my head between my paws and waited.

And waited.

And waited.

"Stop that dratted whining, it's getting on my nerves!" The voice dug into me. "They *said* you were a wonderful family pet... a *dream* to look after..."

I trembled. **Let me out! I want my family.**

Croaky must have sensed my unhappiness, because the stress in her voice disappeared and her breathing was calmer. She was staring at a picture on the wall. "You're right. He's just arrived, he'll be missing them." She held out an open palm. "We're going to be such good friends, aren't we?"

I stood by the door, hoping she'd open it, but she cupped her chin in her hands. "You're very attractive with that dark golden coat and long ears…oh, what's that?" She tugged my fur. "I'll brush you later and get out those burrs and knots." She took my bowls out of the basket, then her nose wrinkled. "Why don't I buy you a nice new basket and surprise Joey when he's back?"

She crouched and clasped her knees. "You'd like that, wouldn't you, dear?" I stared back without blinking, willing her to understand. She pinched my bandana between two fingers, but instead of giving it to me, she dangled it in the air. "We'll keep this somewhere safe, we won't be needing it just now."

A growl rumbled in my throat. I'm not usually a growler, I'm everyone's friend, but not if you're going to take the one thing that's mine… no, it was more than mine, it was mine and Isla's. I jumped and caught it in my teeth, tottering on two paws as she swung from side to side. This was **WAR**. I pulled harder and my claws scratched the floor. Then, suddenly I'd won.

Croaky was facing the picture again, taking deep slow breaths. "Yes, I know, Arthur, it's his first day."

I lay, guarding my treasure until I heard the crackle of packaging. I arched my neck as a delicious smell hit my nostrils.

"Aha, so you *do* like treats!"

I opened my mouth and snatched the meaty chew bar. When I looked up, she'd gone. I heard slurpy footsteps and tracked her to a room with a sofa facing a fireplace. Croaky held my bandana at arm's length in front of a cabinet with a sloping lid. She opened the top drawer and the bandana disappeared.

"Sit down, dear," she said in a gentle voice.

I understood **SIT** but she'd just attacked me. I want to please humans, but sometimes they aren't clear and you have to second-guess them.

A gush of hot breath tickled my whiskers. "It's alright, you'll soon learn the ropes." She stared into the distance. "I left home too — *had* to."

I sensed a deep well of sadness flowing into me as she held out her arms. When she patted me, I wagged my tail. **You get away with a lot if you wag your tail. You can make humans do things they don't want to.**

She smiled. "My name is Maud Mandeville. It's

pronounced Man-de-VILLE. I'm not like Cruella, though!" Dark holes appeared either side of large front teeth as her mouth opened wide. She cackled like a crow, three loud caws. "Unless of course, you misbehave…"

I had no idea what she was talking about, but she croaked again so I tried to look interested, head on one side. When she reached out again, I jumped up with both paws to say hello and she stumbled backwards into a chair, hitting her head. Pins pinged off her hair ball and it tumbled into stringy strands.

"You… you…" She didn't finish what she was going to say but she didn't look happy at all. She certainly didn't seem to find it funny like Isla and Harry did when I bounced at them. My tail stopped wagging. I heard crackly wheezing as she picked up the pins. She scooped up her hair and twisted the strands around one finger to make a tight ball, then stuck the pins in her head. **Weird.**

My legs tensed when she picked her stick, but it wasn't a weapon, more of a third leg. "Would another snack calm you down? I've forgotten what it's like to have a dog around the house." Her neck dipped lower like a bird listening for a worm. "Not that I've ever had a puppy — my old Jasper was a rescue dog and he was such a faithful friend.”

She reached past me and two glass doors swung open to reveal a table and four chairs. I trotted after her, hoping she’d take me home, but instead, she touched the wall above the sideboard and two tiny windows popped out. A wonderful smell wafted towards me and I realised I was hungry. **To be honest, food is one of my hobbies and I spend a lot of time thinking about it.**

Croaky clasped her hands. “We’re having beef bourguignon tonight to celebrate your arrival. All that talk about *Five-a-Day* is a bit overrated if you ask me.” Her eyes twinkled. “And I made scones fresh this morning…” She reached through the hole, then grunted. “Drat. Wait here and I’ll fetch the plate.”

When she left, I leapt onto the sideboard. Could I get through this gap? **Yes, easy peasy.** I did a cool jump and landed on the kitchen table, and snatched a scone. My tongue caught the crumbs trapped on my whiskers, then I dived in for another yummy treat. Mmm, this was a

Great Gulpy Guzzle!

My ears pricked. I looked up. A monster was racing

towards me waving a stick.

"NO!" The word was a command like STOP and SIT and the hard tone made my fur prickle.

I thought it was a clever trick squeezing through that hole. **Better duck under the kitchen table if she's in a mood. Better still, get out of here!**

Light streamed through the fuzzy glass in the back door and I smelt fresh grass. But it was shut. The kitchen led to a room with slits of light all around. The curtainy things swayed when I nosed them and glimpses of green appeared. I was trying to find the way out, when Croaky thundered in and cornered me. "Don't touch the blinds!" The thin papery slats slid apart to reveal a wall of windows. And the garden. "There, that's better, we'd better keep them open."

There's the gate! I pounced at the glass door, but Croaky pulled me back. "Sorry for shouting, but blinds are fragile, and you really mustn't climb through the hatch." She patted her chest and puffed out. "At least you appreciate my food. Come along, dear, don't dilly dally."

Her anger had vanished, so I followed her to the Fire Room while she kept mumbling. Her shoulders squeezed and touched her ears and she cawed again. Humans have strange ways of laughing. Dogs just smile with their tongues hanging out and we wag our tails.

I glanced around. One window. Two ways out.

I knew how to get into the kitchen from the Table Room, but the front door was closer and Isla might be waiting outside. Croaky wasn't watching: this was my chance. I dashed down the hall and sprang at the door, growling in frustration.

THUD!

A shadow loomed. My nostrils twitched as the smell of festering fish swam all over me. The stick smacked the floor and clouds of dust flew up. I spun around and saw popping eyes and scary teeth. Her stick was close to my feet. Too close. I clawed the door harder, trying to push it open. **Come on, open!**

Another shout. Croaky scooped me against her spongy chest, her face inches from mine. "Look at what you've just done! You've scratched my lovely oak door that was Arthur's pride and joy." She pulsed with energy and her heart boomed. I wriggled, but couldn't get free.

Sandals slapped the floor as she marched to the stairs, then she twisted a knob and a cupboard door swung open. I squirmed out of her grip and tumbled to the ground, but the stick shot out, blocking me. "Get in! And stay there until you can behave."

I didn't like this game. Games should be fun with racing and chasing, not shut in a dark room. I howled for help. **Let me out!** My chest heaved and my tongue lolled out like I'd been running for miles, paws powering over the sand.

I want to go home. Isla, where are you?

4. Bandit Bolts for Freedom

The door creaked and a face loomed closer, glinting in the brightness. "So, have you learned your lesson?"

I blinked. Where was I? Huge eyes in huge glasses were staring at me. Then I remembered. Isla's family left me with this croaky stranger.

Why? What have I done wrong?

A wobbly arm reached out and I shrank against the wall. "There's no need to be frightened, you just need to know some house rules." Her mouth stretched wider. "Dinner's in the oven, so let's wander down to the village."

DINNER! That's more like it. I bounced around Croaky's ankles as she walked to the kitchen. My gaze flicked to the bin. Smells were buzzing around it like flies. I pawed the pedal, but the rustle of a lead stopped me in my tracks. I was there in an instant, ears pricked, tail wagging. **Let's go!**

She clipped on my lead, and I smelt Isla all over again and my heart pounded. Was Croaky taking me back to my family? I let Croaky take me outside and as she rummaged in her handbag, I saw my basket, perched high on a tall bin. A rubbish bag was flapping inside it, wafting a mass of tempting scents. If she wanted to give me dinner in bed, I'd be up for it, but how did she expect me to get up there, I'm not a squirrel.

I needed to try to get my basket down to a more sensible height, so I pawed at the bin.

The rubbish bag rustled and a sharp pointed snout poked out. "Oy, stop sniffing around 'ere, mate." The rat's long whiskers twitched. "This is my stash."

I growled. "Get out of my basket. Or I'll snap you in two!"

"Oh yeah? I'd like to see you try!" The brown rat arched up on hind legs revealing his light grey belly. My hackles rose and I barked.

Croaky turned around and tugged the lead. "Don't you *want* to go for a walk?"

Oh yes, WALK! Part of me still wanted to root out the rat, but **WALK** was the magic word and I could smell freedom. I trotted after Croaky and she opened the gate.

"That's a good boy."

I sniffed the air and set off down the hill. Almost immediately, an interesting scent called me. I headed towards the wall, nose to the ground, tracking pee spray. **Whoa, that's strong. I need to meet this dog; he might be able to help me find Isla.**

The lead pulled me back. "Slow down! I'm not an Olympic runner!"

Perhaps it was wiser to go at her pace. The footpath sloped past more houses, then flattened out near a large green area. Cars were parked beside a row of stone cottages with windows watching the field. On the grass, children were swinging into the air with screams of laughter. I strained towards them, but Croaky stopped at a tall red box.

"I'd better post that letter; the NHS keeps pestering me about my heart." She slid a letter into its mouth and the box ate it.

We crossed the road to a bench where she unclipped my lead. "Do your business, but come straight back, mind."

FREEDOM! I raced towards the playpark. The swings squeaked as children sailed up and down. My heart beat faster, then my tail fell. Not Harry or Isla. I turned away and trotted to a tree and lifted my leg.

And heard a scream. "Ugh! That dog's doing a massive pee."

Something whistled over my head and bounced on the grass. Instinct took over and I dashed after the ball and two lads ran after me, snapping at my heels. One overtook and dribbled the ball towards the trees on the far side of the field. I danced around him, my legs springy, eager to play.

A high-pitched whistle sounded.

I skidded to a stop. The football launched into the air and the boys sped towards it. The noise screeched again. But it wasn't the same pitch as Dad's whistle and it was hurting my ears. I darted into the trees, straining to catch my family's scent, but other smells masked it: salty chips, sweet wrappers and tangy cans of drink. More whistling. Fainter now. And children's laughter. Then in the distance, water.

Water means the sea. And Isla!

I headed along a spongy path between the trees and the trickling grew into a rushing sound. Below me wasn't a little stream as I'd hoped, it was a murky green river. I love water, just not swimming. Waves rush at you and get in your eyes and snout. I darted up and down, looking for a way across, but there wasn't a line of rocks to clamber over.

So I dipped a paw in the water and slithered in. My paws slipped on the slippery stones and I couldn't touch the bottom. I splashed harder, trying to keep my head up, but water swirled around me, pulling at my fur. It wanted to drag me down and swallow me up.

GO BACK!

Using all my strength, I fought my way to the bank. I climbed out, a shrunken slopping mess, and shook my frustration over the tufts of grass.

A shriek of laughter reached my ears. This gave me hope. Perhaps there was another place to cross the river, maybe there was a bridge somewhere — I had to get to the sea. I splodged up the path, leaving a wet trail and dripped through the trees onto the field.

Another ear-splitting whistle.

I glanced at the boys. They were staring at the woman waving her stick and holding two fingers to her lips. Croaky whistled again, then hobbled towards me.

"There you are, I thought I'd lost you. Ooo, you're

soaking wet. Did you fall in the river? You poor poppet, anything could have happened."

I stood and shivered, teeth chattering. Then she was rubbing my fur and shaking the water off me. I was desperate to find Isla, but right then, I needed all the comfort Croaky could give me.

"Let's get you warm and dry again. We can't have you catching your death out here, can we? Best be getting home, my lovely, you'll be safe there."

Back at the house, she put a blanket beside the fire and cuddled it around me.

"I've promised to look after you and I can't have you running off like a wild bandit. What would I tell your family if you got lost?" Her fingers danced on my head, making my fur tickle. "I know, while you're here, I'll call you Jasper and perhaps you'll behave." She patted my back. "We'll be good friends, won't we Jasper?"

Jasper? Who's Jasper? My name is Bandit and I run like the wind.

But when we went out that evening, I wasn't let off the lead. She extended it to its fullest length, but I wasn't free. She scooped up my mess with a poop scoop, then we were home again.

No, not home. Home was somewhere with salty spray that tingled my tongue. Somewhere with waves that gurgled and splashed. I was used to rough wooden floors at the cottage and a door that opened in two parts, not a solid front door that shuddered shut. But I'd found out one thing: the way to the sea was beyond the river.

I curled up on the scratchy blanket. I missed the children laughing and shouting. And my soft toys. My ears pricked with every sound in case it was Isla. But all I heard was a heavy thud of Croaky as she trudged overhead. I trembled, but there was nowhere to hide.

5. Licky-Platey-Yum-Yum!

I could leap with precision and catch a ball in mid-air; I could snatch a crumb before it spun to the ground; I could land on Isla's lap from a standing position. So I knew I could jump over the gate. The only problem was, Croaky didn't leave me alone the next day and now it was getting dark.

"Wash your hands, dear," she said, "dinner's nearly ready."

DINNER! I wagged my tail. **DINNER** is one of my favourite words.

She smiled. "It's wonderful to have someone to cook for again. I've been on my own for twelve years since poor old Arthur passed away, God rest his soul." She opened the oven and a whoosh of wonderful smells hit me. I skidded into a sitting position and arched my neck.

"Ahha! I'm glad you like meat. Arthur wasn't one for beef — went all vegetarian after he saw that documentary — but I like a good rump steak, and so did

Joey when he lived with us when his poor mother fell ill, and his father was sick with worry…" She sighed. "Martha was my best friend, you know." She closed the oven, then slapped her thighs. "This way."

The fire was jumping and crackling. Either side were shelves filled with books and picture frames. Croaky lifted one off and traced her fingers along the picture. Sadness trickled out of her. A sniff of snot. A tissue was tossed in the flames where it swooshed into sparks.

The glass doors opened and she tapped the table. "Sit here, I won't be a mo."

A few moments later, the windows popped open in the wall and Croaky's face appeared, framed like a picture. There was no way she'd get through there. She must have realised, because she slid the food on the ledge. The meat was screaming at me to take it, but while I was judging my jump, she shuffled back into the room and placed the plates on the table.

"Make sure you eat everything, no leftovers." Her neck bulged as she swallowed. "Then we'll get on like a house on fire."

I was panting like mad. **Where's mine?**

"Wipe your chin, dear, you're drooling." Croaky pointed to the chair opposite hers. "Come along then."

I stood waiting. **Where's my bowl?**

I nosed around and she banged her stick. "Stop slavering. If there's one thing I can't stand, it's slaver."

Why was she snapping? I hadn't done anything wrong. I was relieved when she held onto the table and placed one of the dinner plates on the floor. "There you are, just this once. I'll put on my napkin and then…"

I dived straight in. I could guzzle this all day!

"STOP!" The scary voice was back. "Wait for me."

I hesitated for a second, but when food's there, nothing else matters. I kept my head down until the plate was empty, then looked up and licked my lips.

Mmm, Licky-Platey-Yum-Yum!

The chair legs swayed as she leant back, a hand on her chest. "Disgusting, quite disgusting." She picked up a little cloth and flapped so hard that her hairball frayed at the edges. "You've put me right off my dinner."

DINNER! A jumble of delicious smells was above me, so I scrambled onto the chair and eyed her plate.

She swiped the wispy strands behind her ears. "That's better, you've decided to eat at the table with me.

Now sit down and mind your manners."

I skated across the shiny table towards her food, but her forearms slammed down either side of the plate. And what do you do if there's danger? **RETREAT!** I jumped onto the floor and darted to the back door. The walls crowded in on me, and the air was heavy like thunder. Croaky tucked a stray hair behind her ear, and I watched every tiny movement, wondering if she was about to seize her stick. She took a step forward. I dodged.

"Jasper, come back here!" She lurched forward, but I hid under the kitchen table.

Hah, you can't catch me!

A gush of hot air tickled my whiskers. "You're tired and teasy, you need to calm down." The long skirt swished, and her sandals slapped across the kitchen. "Perhaps a playtime will stop you being so bouncy and exhausting."

As soon as she opened the back door, I ran for the gate. I could jump this, no problem.

"JAAASSSPER!"

The shout rippled through me, and I lost balance in mid-air and crashed against the top horizontal bar. I clawed, trying to lever myself over, but my nails lost their grip. I fell backwards, swivelling onto my feet. Ouch, a splinter. I wanted to bite it out right away, but Croaky was walking towards me. I launched myself at the gate, but the splinter dug deeper into my pad. Freedom was so close, but because of the pain, I couldn't jump high enough. And the vertical struts were impossible to climb.

In desperation, I limped around the garden looking for an escape route. High stone walls either side and another fence along the back — the place was a prison. With an oily smell of rats. I followed a greasy trail and found a hole. **That's more like it: a tunnel!**

I scrabbled at the narrow entrance, pawing earth behind me. My ears pricked: a rustling noise near the house. I sped back and saw a plastic bag flapping out of the bin. **Food!** An energy boost is a good idea before an escape. I pounced, then felt a sharp pain.

Two round pink ears popped up then Rat's sharp nose peeped out of the bag. "Oy! Watch it mate."

"No, you watch it!" I slammed my paws against the bin. "You nipped my ear."

"Well, you nearly bit my head off."

I growled my most menacing growl, but Rat just sat on the bin, chewing a lump of meat. "Hey, I wanted that,"

I snarled.

"Tough!"

I head-butted the bin and a shower of tasty scraps flew down. **Mmm, there's so much choice! Roast potatoes...juicy carrots...blobs of gravy...**

I dived in, then heard a grizzle of anger. "Jasper, that's disgusting!"

Thankfully, Rat chose that moment to jump down, his long tail flying behind him. Croaky shrieked and ran, her skirt flapping. Rat winked and nibbled a roast potato. "It's a feast tonight."

WHACK! Something whizzed past us, skidding on the grass. "*Vicious Vermin*, can't abide 'em!"

"Rubbish shot," said Rat. He raised his eyebrows. "She often throws those tins at me. I could tell you a tale or two about her. What's your name?"

"Bandit." My hackles rose and I stared at his sharp teeth. "But I don't need your help."

"Suit yourself." And with a flick of his whippy tail, he ran low over the grass and disappeared. Ignoring the pain in my paw, I sprinted to the gate and braced my back legs, preparing to launch.

"JAAASSSPER!"

A can smashed off the gate, splattering stray baked beans. Don't retaliate, I told myself, but my instincts kicked in and I barked at the monster.

"That's right, come to Mummy. I'd never forgive myself if anything happened to you." Croaky's arms were wide, and the stick reached even wider, touching my haunches. She herded me inside where I tried, once again, to plan my escape. Which is hard when you're an **in-the-moment** kind of guy.

I spent ages licking and nibbling my paw trying to get the splinter out. Then I scouted around the kitchen looking for food. Scrumptious smells were hovering behind a thin door, so I nosed it open. The tiny room had shelves all around and a high window with a wire grill. Croaky's bag was in the corner and my lead was hanging on a hook. I stood on hind legs and peered over the cold worktop. Stacks of bottles and jars. Apples and oranges. And a yummy cake. But it was stuck in a tin.

When I'm bored, I chew things. This time it was chair legs. And that got me into big trouble. Croaky burst into the kitchen and her yell nearly burst my eardrums.

Then she stalked to the cupboard and sank her teeth into the cake. I knew she was angry, but when food is there, you've got to try, haven't you? So I begged for a slice. But she pushed me away and jammed down the lid. I tucked my tail between my legs and hid under the table.

When Croaky finally let me into the garden, moths were flitting around the glow from the kitchen window. She was holding a weapon. The handle swung back and I flinched, but the metal end landed in her other hand with a slap.

"It's a proper job, if I say so myself." A beam of light shone on the path. "Follow me." We crunched down to the fence where strange, criss-cross shapes now loomed and stuck up at different angles. The result looked like one of Harry's drawings with scrawly lines everywhere.

She gave a rasping laugh. "Like it? I'll just hammer in this last plank." A pungent salty odour hit me as Croaky raised her arm and hit the fence with the weapon. My nostrils were twitching so fast, I felt dizzy. I mean, it's a gift to have a great sense of smell, but sometimes you don't want to use it.

I backed away and bumped into something hard.

The curved pot was taller than me, and a similar pot stood on the far side of the gate. Like guards.

When I sniffed the plant, Croaky wagged her finger. "I wouldn't, it's prickly. I bought these pyracantha as the garden centre called them *to scratch a thief*." She flicked a spike with her thumb and middle finger. "Perfect for keeping intruders *out*..." Her eyes glowed, "and you *in*. You gave me a real fright earlier, you really did. We can't have you running off, can we, poppet?"

I glared at the plants. **You just wait, I'll find another way to escape.**

6. Can't Catch Me

We're running along the beach. The sand is shimmering, and Isla's hair is flying. I'm racing and bounding and leaping and jumping beside her. Then we stop and collapse in a tangle of legs. I lick her salty face and she giggles and wipes it with her hand. I jump up and dash around her, wanting a game. She picks up a stone. Her shoulder lifts as she pulls back her arm. I focus on her beautiful eyes, watching every tiny change of expression. My legs quiver, waiting. The stone flies into the waves. I run after it and duck my head in. Then I'm racing back and dropping the stone on the beach, and wagging my tail, proud I've found it.

Isla's eyes are bright, she's sparkling with fun. She tosses the stone a little way and I bound over to get it. My back legs dig in and I claw the sand, my front paws whizzing faster and faster. Grains are showering behind me, scooting through my paws, but the stone keeps shifting. And the hole is getting wider and deeper.

Isla ruffles my fur, her hand warm on my back. I look up, panting, and she laughs, her cheeks crinkling. "Bandit, you're like a mole tunnelling backwards!" My tongue lolls with exhaustion, but I'm happy. Her laugh is love. It says I'm me and you're you, and I love being here with you. So I keep digging, my sandy tail wagging against her legs, anything to please her. A giggle of joy flies around us. "Bandit, you're laughing, too, I know you are! I wish we could stay like this forever."

Then suddenly we're running again, racing in and out of the water before the waves can catch us. It's the best tail wagging fun! I'm jumping with great bouncing bounds and Isla's in front of me. I can't see her face, so I run faster, harder, soaring through the air.

And I land with a hard jolt. My paws hurt. I'm alone. It's just me and the waves and the vast empty beach. Isla's calling, but I can't see her. The seabirds are crying, their voices blending in the air. But mist is stealing over the water and eating up the beach... The light is dimming... everything's fading...

🦴

I blinked. Croaky was staring at me, big round glasses

flashing light in my eyes. She reached down to stroke my head. "It's alright Jasper, you were dreaming. Your paws were twitching, and your eyelids were flickering like a lightbulb that's about to pop."

I looked around in confusion. **Where's the beach gone? And Isla? She was calling me; it was so real.**

Croaky yawned stale coffee fumes, then opened the back door. The higgledy-piggledy fence looked even worse in the daylight and sharp prickly wire was coiled around the top of the gate. There was no way I'd get over it now.

"She's really screwed up — look at the shed." Rat held his tail aloft and tiptoed over a jagged splinter, then stared at the corner of the garden.

"What shed?" All I could see were two garden chairs and a pile of sawdust.

"Exactly. She's only gone and demolished it. She kept bird seed in there and it was a lifesaver in winter."

I didn't want to talk to a rat, but he might know the way to the cottage. So, I kept eye-contact and restrained my quivering urge to chase him. "Perhaps that's why she got rid of the shed."

Rat shook some specks off his tail. "I think it's *your* fault. She did this to stop you getting out."

"No, it's Croaky's fault for keeping me prisoner."

"Croaky?"

"Her voice croaks and she laughs like a crow." I tried to imitate the sound, but the caws came out as throaty barks.

Croaky appeared like magic. "Jasper, did you call?"

"Jasper?" said Rat.

"Don't ask," I said, but he'd already gone.

A car horn tooted. A man's voice. "Are you Maud Man-Devil?"

"Man-de-VILLE!"

When Croaky said this, the man stepped back and nearly dropped the boxes he was clutching to his chest. I hoped she wouldn't beat him with her stick. But she held onto my collar and opened the gate. "Please come in."

I sniffed the air, taking in the man's smell. It reminded me of Dad's spicy cooking. As he crunched up to the house, I raced to **Greet the Feet**, running around his ankles and wagging my tail.

He put the parcels on the doorstep, then knelt to stroke me. "Hello Gorgeous, I haven't seen you before." I rolled over. Ok, so I'm not the best guard dog, but everyone likes a good tickle. I only got up when Croaky joined us. She was smiling now, but I needed to warn him that she might flip. So I started to bark.

Help! Sometimes she turns into a monster, and once she shut me in the cupboard!

"Jasper, quieten down, Lovey." Croaky's voice was a little too high; it didn't feel real. She swooped down to pick up the parcels.

This was my chance. I zipped through the man's legs and paused for a goodbye stroke, and he lifted me into his arms. Perhaps he'll take me to the cottage?

To my horror, he handed me back. **No, don't leave me!**

Croaky herded me inside then she stabbed the nearest box with a pair of scissors and ripped off a stream of tape. "Ooo, look Jasper, it's your tartan cushion."

Soon the hall was full of empty boxes. There was a hard basket where you could rest your head and a scratchy basket that smelt of grass. She put this in the Fire Room and tapped it with her stick. "Sitting Room — got it?

I hadn't a clue what she was on about, but she gave

me a strawberry tart when I sat in the basket, and it was

Gobble-Amazing!

She rolled a finger down her lips. "Perhaps I should have ordered another basket for the conservatory? Remind me will you, Jasper?" Her eyes sparkled. "You're going to look really smart and give Celia Trout's poodle a run for her money."

The cushion felt cosy, but it didn't smell like mine. Just then, I heard crashing and smashing. I leapt onto the armchair and looked out of the window. **My basket! A machine was eating it!**

Then I saw Rat. He was creeping along the flowerbed watching the bin trundling back through the gate. The lorry-with-the-jaws rumbled down the road. I couldn't see any more because my breath steamed up the window.

"Get off the chair!"

Why was Croaky shouting again? I jumped down, puzzled; I thought I was allowed. Desire to escape was burning me up. I lapped my water with noisy splashes then stood by the back door, but Croaky didn't get the hint and kept staring at a flat screen on her knees.

"The wretched thing always takes so long to…" She

hit it. "Ahha….this is the one. It'll suit your ginger coat." Her eyelids narrowed. "Oh yes, and we'll need a Tangle Tamer..." My fur bristled as she touched me. "When Amazon comes again tomorrow, I'll start taming this mop."

I ran to the door. **I need a pee!** I wasn't joking; some might have oozed out.

"Wait!" Croaky did a skippity hop and flung open the door. I was so upset my basket had gone that I peed against the bin.

Rat looked gloomy. "Thieving Rotters: they've nicked all our food again." His whiskers twitched. "Look out, I can smell *The Stick*, she's on the warpath!"

I raced after Rat and he swirled around, his tail whipping past my legs. "Why don't you escape, if you don't like it here?"

"What d'you think I'm doing?"

"Oh yeah, like I can see you sailing over the gate!"

"I tried, but my paw hurt."

"Poor liddle paw!" Rat raised an eyebrow, mocking me, then slithered into his hole.

I pounced at the entrance and began digging, showering the earth behind me. **I can do this! It's like**

sand on the beach. I'll soon tunnel out.

SMASH! A branch showered me with leaves. Croaky poked her stick into the hole and stumbled forward onto her knees. "Where's the wretched rat tunnelling to, Australia?"

I wanted to get into the tunnel, but her stick was in the way. And her stick was like fire. There was a squeak behind us, and Rat's black eyes gleamed in excitement. "Oy, can't catch me!" He winked and skidded under Croaky's skirt.

"*Ahhhhhh!* It's in my *knickers*!" she screamed, whacking her thighs.

It was one of those times when you know you shouldn't look, but it was so funny I couldn't help it. Rat streaked under the bush and Croaky ploughed after him, smashing branches either side.

"Where's the nasty *menace*? When I find it, I'll make it into *mincemeat*! I'll slice off its tail like *The Three Blind Mice*!"

I had to see this! I jumped over the flattened branches and saw Croaky leaning over the green tub, her skirt hitched up. Not a pleasant sight, but Rat had caused a diversion, and I wasn't complaining.

Empty cans fired at Rat, and to be honest, I didn't know whose side I was on. Croaky rubbed her hands and obviously thought she'd won. "The tomato soup was a cracking shot!" She hobbled inside, then her breathing went ragged, and spit sprayed my whiskers. "Your paw prints are all over the kitchen floor!"

My ears wafted with the force of her sigh. I quivered in alarm, but instead of raising her stick, she patted my head. "Never mind. At least that's the last we'll see of the vermin."

I wished she'd stop rabbiting on, so I could get back to digging. Then another thought struck me. **If Rat knows a secret way into the garden, he also knows a way out. He can help me escape!**

Everyone knows rats are greedy creatures and they like doing their own thing. I just had to be sneakier than Rat and find a way to persuade him.

7. Finding a Friend

Gradually, I became used to the smell in the house, but I never liked it. Croaky's musky scent clung to my fur, so when she let me out each morning, I kicked the sky — right, left, right, left — then jumped up and shook all over. There's nothing like a good shake to feel better.

Or the sound of a car engine.

I flattened my body and peered underneath the gate, eager for my first glimpse of Isla. The vehicle spluttered, then the door opened. **Oh no, cheesy toes!** A swish of pink knickers. As Croaky levered herself out, a shiver shook my body.

She clicked her fingers. "Don't worry. Arthur's old tank is a bit rusty, but it'll get us to the Pamper Parlour. Jump in!"

The car was a wild animal, crouching then pouncing. I nearly puked up my breakfast, but just in time, we stopped. Outside, there were no familiar smells, no seabirds, just traffic whizzing past tall buildings. Which way was home? I wriggled, trying to slip my collar, but Croaky yanked me through a doorway.

Where I smelt dogs and cats. And **FEAR**.

We were in a large room with two other animals. A cat was trapped in a cage which rested on a man's lap. It peeped out and mewed. The other was a poodle on a lead, held by a woman who smelt of those massive flowers that Mum buys — the ones with pollen that tickles my nose. She looped her handbag over her arm, its shiny chain tinkling as she tottered towards us on clickety-click shoes. I eyed the pointed heels nervously and whisked my tail before it was pinned down.

The poodle's white fur was wild and curly, the way I like it. I glanced at her. "Hi, I'm Bandit." She nosed around me, but when she sniffed my backside, I shivered and pulled away. Some things are private.

"Ooo, a bit precious, are we?" she said. "I'm just saying hello. I'm Polly."

I looked nervously around the room. "What is this place?"

Polly arched her neck. "The grooming parlour. Where we get a make-over: usually a cut and blow-dry."

"You're already pretty," I said, gazing at her thick

white fur.

"This old coat?" She stared down her snout. "Wait until you see my latest style. Spike Feet always brings me here, it's my favourite place."

I glanced at her human who'd sat down and was smoothing her tight skirt above her knees. "Mine's the beach. I need to find my family. Do you know a cottage by the sea?"

Polly put her head on one side. "We sometimes go to our beach hut."

"With a door that opens in two parts?"

She raised an eyebrow. "*Two* parts? Doors don't have two parts."

"Mine does. When the top half's open, you can smell the salty air, it's the best place in the world."

"So why aren't you with your family if you like it so much?"

"They went away and left me with *her*." I turned my head to Croaky, but when I looked back, Polly was being led into another room. I started to shake. I didn't like this place: dogs disappeared. I hid under Croaky's long skirt. It smelt musty like the cupboard, but the fear in the room was worse.

Croaky wriggled to the edge of the seat so I had to move. I sat beside her, and she tapped her fingers on her knees.

Spike Feet said something then dipped into her bag and held out a small sweet. Mmm, it smelt

Yumitty-Scrumitty!

I arched my neck and gave a really good sniff, so she'd know I wanted the sweet, but she passed it to Croaky. The wrapper crackled and I heard slurpy chewing.

Then the door opened. "Jasper Mandeville?" said a man.

"Come on, that's us." Croaky peered at a label on his apron. "Damien, aren't you rather young?" When the man took my lead, she started to pant. "Can't I come in with him, it's his first time?"

He shook his head. I didn't know who was more worried, Croaky or me. **Make this time count, find an escape route**, I told myself as he closed the door.

He lifted me onto a table and clipped my collar onto a harness. His voice was kind, but a tickly whizzy buzzing swept over my fur. That was bad enough, but I protested when he lifted my tail and started clipping around it.

Hey, stop that! I'm not nipping your hair and biting bits off, am I?

Then he led me into another room and strapped a thick coat under my belly. My legs trembled. Once I go down that ramp, waves will rush and tumble over me. He murmured encouragement as he led me into the water. I lurched towards the side of the pool, but he pulled me back. The ramp was beneath my feet.

Now get me out of here!

He threw a ball, and I watched it bob up in the water. I was tempted but I backed up the ramp, hoping to find the way out. Instead, he turned me around. "Go on, Jasper, you know you want to." He gave me a little push, then I kicked out, eyes on the ball. Isla would sometimes throw a tennis ball and she'd scream with laughter as the waves chased us back. I paddled to the man and the ball was wrestled out of my mouth.

SPLASH! It was bobbing around again.

If only I was on the beach with Isla. How would I ever find it again? But right now, I had to get that ball. I launched out and bubbles of joy gurgled around me. **When you have sparkles inside you, you can't**

make a run for it, you need to enjoy the moment.

He laughed. "Well, you certainly like water, Jasper. Next time, I'll take off your life jacket." I skidded down the ramp and he attached my harness to the wall. Soapy stuff slurped and my nails skidded on the floor. Then a storm of fluttery air shook my fur.

After all this pampering, it was too late to escape. But I did learn something important: **I could swim!** A joy I'd never known had been waiting there all the time.

Back in the big room, a dog was standing beside Spike Feet at the desk. Thin as a whippet with puff balls on her head, feet, and the tip of the tail. I couldn't stop staring. "Polly, what have they done to you?"

Her tail dropped. "Don't you like my new look? It's the in-thing this year."

"It's very…different." Gone was her curly coat, she looked naked.

She stared at me. "Well, your new silky look may be smart, but your fur will trail on the ground — you'll be dirty as soon as you step outside."

"Good, I like dirt!"

Polly rolled her eyes like she'd just stood in a cowpat. "My coat would be ruined."

"You'd still look stunning," I said. Then I realised that she was…**stunning**. I just preferred the wilder look.

"Thanks." Polly lifted a paw and hid one eye. She knew all the tricks, this one. She faced me, fluff balls on the ground. "Want to know what I found out?"

I whined eagerly. She glanced at Croaky. "I've seen your human before. Spike Feet knows her. They're planning something."

"How d'you know?"

Polly's whiskers twitched. "Body language. Look how they're nodding. But I think Spike Feet wants to leave — see how she's touching her handbag and edging away?"

"I need to do that," I said.

"What, carry a handbag?"

I wagged my tail. Polly was teasing, as if she liked me now.

'No silly, edge away from Croaky's cheesy sandals…and the stick.'

Polly nodded sympathetically, "Honestly, she's got no idea when it comes to fashion. But at least she doesn't have pointed heels like my human. I'm always on the lookout for those shoes in case she treads on me."

I glanced at the poodle. "So you understand. Will you help me escape?"

Polly gazed at me with deep brown eyes. "Well, I guess if Spike Feet brings me over to your house, I could be a distraction."

"How?"

"Easy when you look like this." She rose to her full height and the furball on her head puffed out and light shone around her like the sun was shining.

I didn't think I'd like the Pamper Parlour, because washing and preening isn't really my thing. I'm more of a **run-on-the-beach-with-the-wind-in-your-hair** kind of dog. I only went so I could escape. Ok, I admit it, I didn't have a choice. But I'd made a friend, and she was going to help me get back to Isla.

When Croaky opened the garden gate, a parcel was lying on the doorstep. She hopped around like a little kid. Before I knew what was happening, my old collar had slipped onto the ground and a new one dug into my throat. I wriggled and twisted but couldn't bite it off.

Croaky's glasses slipped down her nose, and she

pushed them up with a finger. "Look at your shiny new tag, Jasper. Bandit's too rough a name for a pretty little thing like you." I squirmed and snatched my old collar. She laughed and grabbed the other end. "Alright, let's have a tug of war; I haven't done this for years!"

Oh, so this is a game!

With a growly grizzle, I twisted from side to side. She fought back, wrestling with both hands, then there was a tinkling sound. Croaky scooped up the tag, jingling it above me. She stalked into the Fire Room and opened the top drawer of the cabinet.

I smelt my bandana and ran towards Croaky, but she slammed the drawer shut. I jumped and scratched, trying to claw it open. Her breathing was wild, she was going to slash me to pieces.

WHACK!

I shrank under the table, trembling, but she didn't attack again. Something had changed. The room felt lighter; the cloud of anger had vanished. Feet dragged across the room and a chair creaked. I peeped out — just a little, I'm not crazy. Croaky was rocking back and forward with her head in her hands, making strange mooing noises. Was she sick?

While I was assessing my chance of getting through the door or the window (nil), the mooing stopped, and she rubbed her eyes. She shoved her glasses back on and her chin jutted out. "No, I have to, he needs to learn." The stick jabbed at my collar forcing me out, then arms grabbed me. A few seconds later, I was facing the cupboard. "Go and cool off for a few minutes. I know you're still a puppy, but you *must* learn not to scratch the furniture."

Silence. No creaking, singing pipes like the cottage by the sea. No children playing hide and seek. My throat hurt and I hated the new collar. I nosed around, tripping over a loopy hose. Dust tickled my nostrils, so I curled up in a corner and whimpered for Isla.

But it wasn't a young girl's voice that I heard, it was Croaky. "Hello? Who's that?" Her voice was sharp, like a whip.

Was someone else here? I sniffed the tiny gap under the door but there were no new smells. Her voice suddenly turned warm and happy.

"Oh, it's you, Joey! How lovely to hear from you… No, there's nothing wrong. He's taken to me like a duck to water…Yes, he's eating me out of house and home!…

No, you don't need to transfer any...You're very welcome, anything to help. How was your journey? Not too hot I hope."

There was a pause then Croaky laughed. "No, he's been good as gold. Yes, of course I'll let you know if he's any bother…he's a little poppet, isn't he?"

8. The Escape Committee

I'd only been stuck in the house a short while, but I'd already learned to be wide awake before the stick hit the floor.

"My, that's a loud yawn. You'll wake the dead." Croaky's voice sounded even more breathy than usual. "It's *Friends Friday* today so you'd better look lively, I can't have Celia Trout winning STAR BAKER again. Let's have a quick breakfast, then I can start baking."

I bounded out of the basket, hoping to go outside and start tunnelling right away, but a delicious smell was coming from the kitchen and the air was thick with fatty sizzling oil. Croaky followed me and flapped her hands. "'tis smeechy from those sausages; I got distracted looking at the cake recipes." A chair scraped back. "Sit at the table like a good little boy." I looked at the chair, then at Croaky. "Oh, very well…" she said and lifted me up.

She wants me to sit on the chair. This is fun!

She took two triangles of white material from the sideboard and offered me one. It wasn't tasty so I spat it out. She didn't seem to want the cloth after that, because she flicked it off the table with her stick. Then she stood behind me, pressing the other cloth against my throat. "It's just like tying a tie…"

I broke free, then spun around and looked at Croaky. **What's this supposed to be: my new bandana?** It didn't smell of Isla, so when Croaky went to fetch my food, I gripped the cloth in my teeth and tugged it off.

She sighed. "Never mind, perhaps you don't like wearing a napkin?" A plate of sausages was placed in front of me. This was way better! I opened my mouth in anticipation. You can't wag your tail when you're sitting down, but inside, my whole body was wagging.

"Lesson one…" Croaky held up a finger. "WAIT!"

She walked around the table, while slaver dripped down my jaws. The meaty deliciousness was screaming: **Eat me, I'm the yummiest thing you've ever tasted!** She wafted a cloth over her face. That must be the signal. I dived in. Yum-eeee, it was

Gobble-Gooey-Gorgeous!

The plate was sliding so I stood on the table and put

a paw on it. Clever, eh? Once I'd started eating, it was impossible to stop. I licked my lips, pleased with myself.

"JAAASSSPER!"

Her voice sliced into my ears and rumbled around my head. I jumped down, trembling, but to my relief, Croaky stopped shouting. She was looking at the picture on the wall. "No, don't say it, Arthur — I know." Then she slumped, elbows on table, head in her hands. "If this is what feeding a baby is like, I'm almost glad I never…"

She sounded sad, so I didn't run away. Her eyes started to leak, and her lip wobbled like Dad's had. I rubbed against her leg, and she stroked me. "Aw, are you saying sorry? I'm sorry too. I shouldn't have shouted. Once you've learned how to eat properly, we're going to have so much fun."

She clapped her hands, then pulled them apart with a sticky slurp. "Right, I'll get on with the baking. You go outside." She shooed me into the garden.

Rat was sitting on the tall bin, swishing his tail to balance. "Still here, then?"

I hate sarcasm so I didn't answer. Besides, I wanted to ask him a favour.

"Will you help me dig a tunnel?"

He arched up on his strong back legs. "What's in it for me?"

My whiskers twitched. "Fancy a sausage?"

"And...?"

"Bacon butties?"

Rat's eyes twinkled. "If you want me to mastermind The Escape Committee, I want three meals a day. You dig from this side and if you're any good, our tunnels should join up."

"How long will it take?"

He sniffed greedily. "Get us some stash and we'll see." He swung his tail towards the green tub. "She's rinsed out the tins today. What's the point of putting tins outside if they're completely empty, not even any dregs?" He wrinkled his nose. "I wouldn't live in that house if you paid me, she's a whacko."

I raised an eyebrow. **Look who's speaking!**

Rat narrowed his eyes. "Well, don't take all day. Offers have a shelf-life, you know."

When Croaky opened the back door an hour later, the air sizzled with sweet flavours. I nosed around the kitchen floor licking up crumbs then looked up, hoping for more. She sucked her fingers then sang in a warbly voice.

"Star Baker, Star Baker, Hurray!

I'll beat that Old Trout and be Star Baker today!"

She was fizzing with excitement as she held a wire rack and slid some buns onto a plate. My tail swished against her long skirt, and I held up a paw. When she didn't give a treat, I offered the other paw.

"Ah, what a polite boy. You're saying please, aren't you?" She picked up a bun and gazed at me.

Come on then! I kept tapping her arm, my paws whirring faster to get her attention.

Her lips began to dance. "Well, perhaps this once..."

In one **Gobble Guzzle**, it was gone.

Then I nosed the crinkly cake case that had fallen on the floor. The stick whacked it away. "Don't eat that. Foil goes in recycling — the blue bin."

I ignored her and kept snuffling for scraps.

I'd only just cleaned up when the bell rang. Croaky put the cakes out of reach and went to the door. My nose began to tickle as Spike Feet staggered inside, pulling a huge bag on wheels. The sneezy flower smell ate up the hall as her clickety-click shoes echoed down the corridor.

I didn't want to be spiked, so I squeezed past to greet Polly, racing around her in circles.

Her tail zipped up high. "Calm down, you're making me dizzy. It's taken ages to get here as Spike Feet's brought so much baking."

"Croaky's made cakes, too," I said, looking longingly at the worktop.

Polly glanced in that direction, then looked at Spike Feet who was piling things onto the kitchen table. Each time she took something out of the trolley bag, I dipped my head in. Polly was more polite, but come on, this was a feast! Out came a small tray bulging with food, then several plastic tubs which smelt delicious when the lids squeaked off.

"Maud, what on earth have you been doing to your fence, it's such a …"

"Feat of engineering?"

"I was going to say a mess." Spike Feet pulled something invisible from the tray and crinkled it into a ball. "Dada! Practically perfect, aren't they?"

"So, *you've* tried your hand at scones this week, how lovely." I sensed Croaky wasn't being honest. "Take a seat in the conservatory, Celia. We wouldn't want your ankles to swell up wearing those heels."

Spike Feet stepped into the Glass Room, then she spun around and peered at Croaky's sandals. "Is that cheese I can smell?"

"Er…that must be last night's quiche," said Croaky. "I've just binned the leftovers." Her toes shrank, causing the wide strap of her sandals to bulge. "I'll just get a pretty plate for your scones. Would Polly like a treat?"

Spike Feet crossed her legs. "Only if it's dairy-free."

The women argued about some kind of flat cake Spike Feet had made, but they didn't seem interested in giving any to me so I gazed at Polly. Gone was the fluffball on her head; now it formed a mane down her back. The ball on her tail was teased out like a brush and her legs were silky smooth.

"I wasn't totally happy with Polly's last make-over, so she had a Lion Cut this morning, isn't she beautiful?" gushed Spike Feet, clasping her hands.

There was a loud snort. "So, she didn't chase the cat at the Pamper Parlour?"

CAT! Polly jumped up and raced around the room.

"Why did you say the C-word, Maud?" snapped Spike Feet. "Come to Mummy, Polly-Dolly."

Croaky made a gurgly noise in her throat. "C-word? Oh, you mean *cat*? My Jasper would chase off a *cat* if it dared get in our garden."

CAT! Polly leapt on the chair, her legs shaking.

The high heels raised off the floor as Spike Feet leant forward and adjusted her wing-tipped glasses. "You did that deliberately, Mandeville." She bit into a cake, and as it fell apart, I caught the crumbs in mid-air.

Awesome! My reactions were super sharp but I didn't get congratulated, because she was busy spitting into a tissue. "Four out of ten: your sponge is lumpy."

"I'll give you lumpy!" Croaky pointed to the plate. "Your scones are *two* out of ten; hard as nails."

The high heels clicked together. "Well, your Victoria sponge has a saggy bottom."

"Who are you calling a *Saggy Bottom*, Snootface!"

While the women chirped like birds, I nosed Polly. "I need to get away. Have you found my cottage with the door that opens in two parts?"

"No, we haven't gone to the beach for ages. Maybe your Croaky will take you?"

I glanced at Croaky. "I'm not sure — she seems to think I live here now. Just as well I have a back-up plan

— I'm going to tunnel out of here. I've made a deal with Rat: he's promised to help if I bring him food."

Polly's whiskers twitched. "Never trust a rat. Think outside the box."

"What box?"

"It means think sideways, up and down, wherever — other ideas."

"Oh." I felt stupid.

She raised an eyebrow. "So…?"

Suddenly I knew what to do.

9. The Tunnel

I could still smell traces of Spike Feet when I woke. At least her strong perfume masked Croaky's musky scent. It gave me hope. I could be a master of disguise and escape before she even realised I'd gone! I scouted around the flowerbeds at first light, searching for the best place to start tunnelling. I caught glimpses of Rat — running along the fence, ferreting in the bin — then tracked him to a pile of rotting vegetation where I heard a ratty snore.

"Fine, I don't need your help, I'm working solo today." I tried digging in three places.

STONY. Too painful.

SOLID. Too hard.

LOOSE. Just right.

I set to work, powering my paws.

Then I froze. Croaky was stalking around the garden, prodding with a garden fork. She pierced the molehills I'd just made, thrusting the prongs in deep. I was glad Rat wasn't there. He's not my favourite person, but I don't want him sliced in two.

Croaky scooped up some broken flowers and did her eyelid-narrowing, lip-squeezing thing. I knew I was about to be rumbled, so I put my head on one side and gazed back with big eyes and panting tongue. It's good to cultivate cute expressions, they can get you out of tough situations.

It worked! She patted my head, then propped the broken flowers in the bird bath. "What a clever boy. You're keeping that wretched rodent at bay, aren't you?"

As soon as she went indoors, I pinpointed a better place for my tunnel near the back fence.

SOFT EARTH? Check.

HIDDEN FROM VIEW? Check.

CLOSE TO FREEDOM? Check.

When scrumptious smells drifted across the grass, I headed inside: you need a hearty breakfast before a home run. Croaky tapped a chair, then held out her arms. My tail thumped the carpet. She hovered some salty bacon above me, so I jumped onto the chair to reach it.

She clapped. "Good boy. Isn't this fun!" She held a metal spoon and balanced a sausage on it. "Open wide…"

I tried to focus on her eyes, not the sausage coming towards me, but it was torture.

The smell was powering around me. Pouring into my nostrils. Tingling my tastebuds. Tempting the tip of my tongue. Saying **EAT ME NOW!**

Her eyelids widened. "Get your paws off the plate!" As she shouted, the sausage flew off the spoon and rolled across the table. I dived, the plate scooting past me. *SMASH!* The fried egg did a **Slurpy-Slip** and a gush of **Gloopy-Gooeyness** splashed everywhere.

"Noooo!" Croaky tottered on one foot, then skidded and landed on her bum. She got up on all fours, panting like she'd run along the beach. Her top lip curled as she looked at the gunge oozing down her blouse. Then she faced me, elbows on the table, holding a knife and fork in her fists. Rat was right, she was crazy.

A second later, the weapons clattered on the table. Croaky was staring at a picture propped on the sideboard. "Oh, very well, but he's *not* licking the plate." She turned her stick upside down and putted the broken pieces into the hall. "Good shot, Mandeville."

I'd almost cleared up the yummy mess when the doorbell rang. A hand poked a letter through the flap, and I caught it. **YES!** This was one of my party tricks back home and the children loved it.

Hissy hot breath hit me as Croaky wagged her finger in my face. "NEVER take things out of the letterbox! You could have had his hand off and then where would we be?" She fingered the envelope and her lips lifted. "Ooo, it might be from Joey..." She pulled out a piece of paper, then her shoulders sank. "It's just from the girl."

I couldn't work Croaky out: she was like a gentle wave one minute, then she'd suddenly fire up and come crashing down on me. I nosed her hand, and the paper floated onto the carpet. When I tried to retrieve it, my claws got trapped in her cardigan. She shook me off, so I crept onto the doormat and tucked my muzzle in my fur. I was only trying to help.

How can you know what humans want if they keep changing their minds?

Feet slapped the corridor, then the garden rushed inside, fresh and grassy. I dashed outside to avoid any more of Croaky's anger, and I began tunnelling.

Rat slithered out of a heap of rotting leaves. "You're making a right racket. Can't a guy get any beauty sleep?" He snouted around the earth I'd dug out. "What a mess. You need to learn from the pro."

I growled, spraying soil on his whiskers. "So, where's your tunnel, then?"

With a whisk of his tail, he climbed onto the wheelbarrow handle. "Where's my breakfast, I thought we had a deal?"

I glared at him, then spotted a little round hole near

the compost heap. I bombed over and started to dig, shooting earth behind me. When I came up for a breather, something swooshed over my head and pinged on the fence.

"IT'S THE STICK!" shouted Rat, his pink nose twitching.

I peeped through the bushes. Croaky was holding out her skirt, filling it with cans from the green tub. Rat grinned, then sped towards her like a bullet, veering off at the last moment.

"Get out of 'ere, you *'Orrible Oily Rat*!" A volley of cans spattered the grass. I ducked under the wheelbarrow for safety. Rat's stinky droppings were everywhere. I was so repulsed by his toilet that I didn't hear anything until the ground shook above me.

"Where's the nasty critter, I'll sniff it out…"

BOING, BOING! The shaking in my head was horrible. Then it got worse: the wheelbarrow rose in the air, and I smelt fishy armpits.

"Jasper, what on earth…?" Bulging muscles scooped me up, then I heard loud cawing. "Haha, I've got myself a rat catcher!" She set me down, then grabbed the wheelbarrow handles. Her back creaked as she leant to one side, then the wheelbarrow flew over my head, smashing against the fence.

I was still quivering in shock — I mean, she'd nearly flattened me — when Croaky strode up swinging a heavy spade.

WHACK! WHACK! WHACK!

She dug a trench around the hole, then held her hips and sucked in deep breaths like Mum blowing up a balloon. "Hah! Now to fill in the moat and drown the blighter — I think the hose is long enough." She swung her glasses in the air. "I've had a better idea. Follow me!"

She marched over to some large rocks sticking up between clumps of flowers, then her skirt rode over her knees and her bum nearly touched the ground as she clasped a rock with both hands. "One, two…"

Her cheeks bulged, and her glasses slipped down her nose as she waddled like a crab across the grass. "I'll block the whole area and get rid of those nasty rat holes. That'll teach the *thieving rotter*." She dropped the rock and the ground shuddered.

So did I.

We had Cornish pasties for lunch, and I ate three. I needed energy if I was going to escape tonight: tunnelling's hard work and the hole was only two feet deep. By teatime, it was four feet. Then I struck rock. It took ages to dig around it and it was dark when I was let inside. This time, I remembered to clean my paws so Croaky wouldn't suspect what I'd been up to. I could hardly take my feet off like her, could I?

She squeezed into the armchair and sipped a fiery liquid, and her head drooped onto her chest. I nosed her arm. **Wake up, let me out again!**

"Arthur?" said a blurry voice. She blinked and pushed the glasses up her nose. "Oh, it's you, Jasper. I must have dropped off. Would you like a bedtime story?" I ran to the door and looked back, wagging my tail, but she walked to the bookshelf, not getting the hint.

"I've kept all my old childhood books. You can go places when you read; sometimes it's the only way to escape." Her finger stroked along the knobbly book spines, touching each one. "You can hide in stories and be whoever you want to be." She sighed. "Especially when life is tough, like it was for me as a child."

As she reached for a book, the letter slid off the little

round table. Sniffy excitement leapt inside me. I pounced in front of Croaky and she rubbed her wrinkly forehead.

"Oh, yes, we haven't finished reading it, have we?" She pressed her hands on the chair arm. "I used to love listening to Mother read; those were the best times, snuggled up on the sofa." Another sigh shook her body. "Dear Bandit…blah blah blah…ah yes, this is where I got up to."

> I hope you're ok and not missing me too much. I miss you all the time. Well not quite all the time — there's a cool pool near us and a water slide.

The voice was Croaky's, but a familiar scent was calling me and all I could think of was running like the wind.

> The sand hurts your feet, it's so hot! Have you gone to the beach yet? Dad's given me a challenge of learning all the coves from Port Isaac to Rock because we're going to walk right along the headland when we're back. We'll start from our cottage and walk through Squeezy Belly Alley to the harbour. You might even nick someone's chips again!

"Aw, isn't that sweet?" Croaky stared at me, then at the letter, then at me again. I knew she was saying something without talking and it didn't feel good. Then she dropped the paper in the fire. It sizzled into tiny bits then vanished. I whimpered. Where had it gone?

Her back creaked as she arched her shoulders, then she looked at me and cracked her knobbly knuckles. "Don't worry, Sweetie, you're with *me* now. We may not have the sunshine in Dubai, but we've got each other, haven't we?"

10. No Barking, No Running, No Gobbling!

It was an inspired idea. The wheelbarrow was lying on its back where it had landed, one handle spiking into the ground, wheel in the air. There was a little gap where you could squeeze underneath, it was perfect. Croaky had been working all week and massive rocks were piled against the back fence (the spot I'd earmarked for my escape), so I needed a new base. When she wasn't rubbing smelly stuff into her hands, she patrolled the garden, so we had to be cautious. I say we, but I'm sure Rat had an agenda of his own. I'd brought him titbits every day, but he kept demanding more.

We started the tunnel on a freezing cold day when Croaky stayed indoors. Whenever she let me out — and I developed this cool method of drinking loads, so she let me out a lot — I pretended to sniff around the garden for Rat. When the coast was clear, I'd nip to the back of the wheelbarrow and dive down. My paws ached and my ears clogged up, but who cares about pain when freedom's in sight?

"Inspection Time," said Rat, slithering into the tunnel. He popped back in seconds. "It needs to be way deeper to get under the fence."

I sighed. "How deep's your end?"

"Oh, it's coming on, don't you worry about me."

I raised an eyebrow. "I'll bring a three-course-dinner if you finish your half tonight?"

"What, like yesterday's regurgitated quiche? I don't want your dregs, mate."

Anger made me dig faster, but earth clogged my ears and crumbled into my eyes. I wriggled in fear, trying to avoid it. **The tunnel was caving in!** I only got out by kicking hard with my back legs, then slithering.

Rat stood on hind feet and gestured with his tiny pink paws. "The trick's to *Pace, not Race*. I guess it's a whole different ball game for an animal your size."

I edged forward, feeling irritated. "I'm sorry?"

He jumped onto the wheelbarrow. "I meant well-built. Here's a tip for free: dig an escape hatch and dump the soil there."

"Can't you take it out for me?"

"What do you think I am, a *dogsbody?*"

"Very funny." I grimaced and my jaw muscles ached. "I can't dig *and* make passing places."

"Well, if you don't want my advice…"

This time I burrowed a bit further until the fear got to me. Rat must have heard my wheezy panting because he zoomed down and helped. I was so relieved that I almost licked him — *almost!* He chuckled in a ratty kind of way. "It's all in the head. Believe you can burrow, and you will."

"But it's so dark."

"Duh! It's underground." He brushed past and my fur bristled. "If you really want to know the secret, we burrowers have Night Vision."

"Night what?"

"Instinct and Experience. We store up routes and imprint them on our minds." He rubbed his lips. "I'm peckish. Rustle up a bacon butty, will you?"

"JAAASSSPER!"

Croaky's shout resounded off the wheelbarrow.

"Mummy's calling," said Rat. "Remember our bargain."

Rat's words kept going through my mind: Store up

routes… But what was my route out of here? And how could I find one when I was forced into more training? Croaky kept giving me lessons and I kept failing them:

NO BARKING!

NO RUNNING!

NO GOBBLING!

My lips were already drooling big-time. I mean, what was I supposed to do when she plonked three-course dinners right under my nose, and they smelt so

Scrumlicious!

Croaky wanted obedience, and to be fair, she rewarded me well when I obeyed.

She clapped her hands. "Two taps on the table means you can start eating."

It's so difficult waiting when your taste buds are screaming and you're about to eat chicken chasseur and crispy potatoes. Naturally, I leapt on the table.

"Get down!"

DOWN! I know that word. I jumped on the floor, but she grabbed the scruff of my neck and dumped me back with a whoosh of croaky breath. "Not *down* there, *up* here! We don't eat off the floor, do we?" She sighed. *"What have I done?* I should never have said yes." Her shoulders fell. "But it's been so long without you, Arthur."

Her voice lost its Grr-ness; the picture of the man had magic that made her stop shouting. She ladled some chicken onto my plate, dripping with gravy. "Wait until I take my next mouthful before you do. People don't eat before the king, do they?"

I had no idea what she was talking about, but my senses were on fire. I dived in and licked the plate clean.

"Jasper, that's disgraceful! We do NOT lick our plates."

I wagged my tail. **More please!** I wasn't joking. I needed some more to bribe Rat. Not that I wanted to be friends with a rat, this was strictly business.

Instinct and Experience... I repeated Rat's mantra as I burrowed that afternoon. It kept me sane — if you can call clawing through earth sane. I was disappointed when Rat said the tunnel *still* wasn't deep enough and I needed to dump soil in escape hatches. I looked around and spotted a flowerpot. "Can't we put the soil somewhere else?"

Rat raised an eyebrow. "Wait there." A few minutes later, he returned with a plastic bucket. "Dada!"

"Where did you get that?"

"Four doors down; they have three kids."

It wasn't easy nosing earth into the container, and even harder gripping it in my teeth whilst backing. Rat said he was on **PLANNING** and **STRATEGY**, but it was me who had the brainwave. I dragged the hose across the grass and Rat sawed through with razor sharp teeth. It didn't take long to thread the hose through the bucket handle and when he cut the other end, I wound it around a tree — it's one of my talents: going round and round in circles.

I looked at Rat. "You pull out the bucket when it's full."

"But that's hard work."

"Well, if you aren't strong enough…"

He arched up and flexed his arms, so I slid into the tunnel. I pawed earth into the bucket, then tugged the hose. It didn't move. I tipped a bit out then butted the bucket with my shoulder and it inched upwards.

The plan was working!

When I crawled out, we'd done three loads, and I was so thirsty that I lapped all the water in the bird bath.

A piercing whistle. I spotted Croaky shielding her eyes with her hand, so I limped across and lay at her feet. "Ugh, you're covered in mud! I'll get the hose."

A few seconds later, the shriek was so impressive that the kids in the playpark would've heard. "It's been gnawed right through! I bet it was that dratted rat." Heat exploded out of her as she punched the air. *I'm going to tear out its whiskers and fry 'em in oil! I'll slice off its tail and feed it to the ducks!"*

She stamped inside and staggered back with a washing up bowl. Before I'd guessed her plan, she tipped cold water over my head. Then she hooded me with a towel and picked me up. "Come inside, there's a monster with scissor teeth out there!"

That night, I waited until she'd gone upstairs, then I ran to the back door. Energy built inside me as I stared at the handle. One, two… I sprang at the door and the key fell out.

Croaky burst into the kitchen in a swishing flimsy dress. "Jasper, whatever's the matter? Couldn't you sleep?" She was wearing red slippers with fur around the edges, but her feet still smelt of cheese. My whine turned into a yawn, and I curled into a ball, with my paw over my face, trying to hide the smell.

"Had a nightmare, did you, my lovely?" I peeked out and saw Croaky touch her forehead. "I know all about those." Soft hands stroked my back. "Night night, then. See you tomorrow."

As soon as the stairs creaked, I jumped up again. And heard snuffling. "Let us in, will you?" The tip of Rat's tail swished under the door. "Where's my dinner?"

"I couldn't get any."

"Aw, go on, man, I'd die for a bacon butty."

I glanced at the bin. "If you open the door, you can raid the kitchen."

Rat sniggered. "Chuck us some chicken and I'll unpick the lock."

I retrieved some floppy bacon fat from the bin and fed it under the door (well, most of it), then heard disgusting guzzling and burps. "Hurry up Rat, I've got to get away tonight."

A chicken fart oozed through the gap. "Sorry mate, too stuffed now."

"That's gross."

"There's plenty more where that came from. Wait until she makes curry, then you'll get a real wafter!"

"Please, I'll give you more chicken if you break me out."

"Don't you think I've tried twisting the key before?"

"But you said…"

Rat chuckled. "Can't you take a joke?"

I shouldn't have fallen for it. Rat's pink nose peeped out. "See that kink? Tin of Tomato Soup that was — nearly sliced me tail off."

"Serves you right."

"Thanks a bunch. Know how to make friends, don't you?"

"You aren't my friend."

"But I was thinking about it. The last tin she threw almost did me in. I'll scratch her eyes out if she tries it again, I'll bite off her hair-bun, I'll gnaw that 'orrible stick."

"I hate the tapping," I said, "it gives me the creeps." I jumped at the door and the glass shivered.

"W…who's there?" Croaky stumbled into the kitchen, her flimsy dress shaking. "Oh, it's you, Jasper. What on earth are you doing?" She lifted her arms, and the tie-belt came loose, and the frilly things ballooned like they were trying to escape. I knew the feeling.

I heard a squeak outside. "Oy! Is that The Stick?"

Croaky squeaked in an even higher pitch. "Is someone outside?"

I glanced at the key. **Idiot! Why did I do that? Now she's picked it up.**

She passed it from hand to hand. "You tried to warn me, didn't you, Jasper?" she said in a trembling whisper. "I'm so glad you're here, you're a wonderful guard dog. Now I know there are prowlers around, I'll increase my security." She looked into my eyes. "We'll show the rotters, won't we, my lovely? We're the *Dream Team*, you and me."

11. The Whizzy Water Cannon

The tunnel was much deeper than me now. Clawing my way upwards was even harder than digging. How can you turn in a tight tunnel when you like food, like me? Rat said the tunnel was curving too much and I'd end up where I started, but we can't all be rats, can we? And who'd want to be? But at least I was making progress. Not that Rat was helping. He claimed he was focusing on his end of the tunnel; but with no Bucket Buddy, I had to dig out passing places and dump the spare earth there.

It was exhausting, dark and hard to breathe. Horrible tight spaces. When I finally staggered into the light, I'd do long roly polys in the grass. All that digging and climbing and rolling and shaking was enough to make me want to quit. Then the nightmares started.

Fat slugs oozing slime into my ears.

Armies of ants squeezing under my eyelids.

Giant worms about to swallow me whole.

I awoke from the worm nightmare to Croaky whacking pastry. The squelch and bubble didn't sound appetising, so I pawed the back door. She waved me back with the rolling pin, then slid a tray into the oven. Nails drummed on the worktop as she looked out of the window.

"Come on, come on, where are you? I want to set up the water feature before Celia gets here."

The squeak of the gate. Crunching gravel.

Croaky opened the door and I raced up the path, barking. I don't think they liked my welcome, because the gate shuddered shut and a letter sailed onto the grass. I bounded over and grabbed it in my teeth. When I gave it to Croaky, she went all bubbly. "Ooo, is it from…?" She ripped open the envelope and pulled out a piece of paper.

A hiss of breath. Grating teeth. I don't know why Croaky was angry, because a lovely, sweet smell was floating around.

The tramp of feet. Another visitor. Croaky stormed up the path, stabbing her stick in the gravel, and the paper fluttered behind her. I wanted to investigate, but a scrumptious spicy smell was wafting over the fence.

Box Man edged into the garden clutching two parcels. "Hello Gorgeous."

"Ooo, how kind," said Croaky, patting her hair.

"I didn't mean…" He leant away from Croaky. I liked Box Man, but freedom was in sight and this time I wasn't wasting my chance. I did a nifty dodge around Croaky's ankles, but she yanked my collar, dangling me in mid-air. Then bummed the gate shut.

Box Man stammered something, and she spun around, cuddling me against her cardigan. "Don't you worry about Jasper. He's still a pup so he can be daft at times, but he's very friendly and always eager to say hello." Croaky turned all bubbly, chatting in a fast, happy voice. "It's *Friends Friday* and you're welcome to stay. You can judge who's STAR BAKER."

He shuffled backwards. "I'm snowed under, loads more drops to do."

"But we're having lemon drizzle…"

His shoulders pressed against the gate, and he thrust the parcels at her.

"Ooo, is that one the water cannon?" she said. 'It's for the *Thieving Rotters*. A law unto themselves, they are."

The gate slammed and the car roared off.

Croaky scraped her nail along the first box and lifted out a new hose. I pounced on the packaging, angrily ripping it to shreds. If I'd been quicker just now, I could have escaped.

My ears pricked. Croaky had hooked the new hose on the wall, and she was pulling the end across the slabs. She opened the other parcel, then pressed a plastic spiky thing into the flowerbed and attached the hose at the base.

She blew on her hands, then called me. I had a bad feeling about this, but she kept calling so I crept over the grass.

"STAY!" Croaky held up her finger.

I froze in obedience, waiting for a treat. *WHOOSH!* A jet of water hit me. That's what I get for being good? I darted to one side, but it kept firing at me. I retreated, tail between my legs, shivering.

Croaky cawed in delight. "It works! You triggered the motion sensor, Jasper." She rubbed her hands together. "That'll fix the wretches." She was so excited her legs went all jiggly and she bounced on her tiptoes. I didn't even get a rub down, so I rolled on the grass. I was about to give a massive shake, when the **Whizzy Water** soaked me for a second time.

Grrr! What is this thing?

After the door closed, I headed straight for the tunnel. Rat was lying under the wheelbarrow and moist brown droppings were everywhere. I barked to wake him. "I need this space. Can't you go to the loo somewhere else? And why aren't you working?"

"Gerroff, it's bright daylight!" He blinked. "Been for a swim? You ought to be thinking more about food — for *me*, that is. Where's *my* stash? I can get my pickings elsewhere, you know."

I considered giving Rat a knock-out blow, but he scampered out of reach. I chased him across the grass when the **Whizzy Water** jet splattered him, and he skidded back. "This vicious thing spat at me; I got a lung full."

I couldn't help laughing. "It got me too."

"What got you, Bandit?" said another voice.

Polly! I wagged my body from side to side as Spike Feet opened the gate and walked clickety-click down the path. They both side-stepped to avoid brushing against my wet fur.

Polly glanced at me. "Who were you talking to?"

"No one."

Rat's sharp snout poked out from the bushes. "Thanks a bunch." I ignored him and rubbed noses with Polly.

The back door opened and Croaky stood in the doorway, apron flapping. "Drat. I haven't finished the lemon drizzle."

Spike Feet arched her neck trying to see inside. "Bit of a mess, is it?"

Croaky opened her arms, filling the entire doorway. "I thought we'd have a garden party; take advantage of this lovely summer's day."

The food was laid out on Croaky's little table. I licked my lips when Spike Feet dangled a piece of apple pie in two fingers. "Your pastry's a little gooey today, Maud."

"Gooey, is it? Well, your treacle tart's crisped to a cinder!"

I wanted to cut the argument short by fetching Croaky's discarded mail, but Polly got to it first. Spike Feet took the paper and began to read. "I didn't know you wrote poetry."

Croaky's jaw clicked. "I don't."

"Well, take a geek at this." Spike Feet held it close to her face and started to read.

> My dog smiles with his eyes and
> laughs with his tongue lolling out,
> he never shouts or tells you off
> he just wants to be with you.

The smell of sweat gushed towards me as Croaky lifted her arm. "Give me that!"

"Aw, you don't need to be embarrassed, it's lovely." Spike Feet ignored the frantic flapping and kept reading.

> His ears are soft as silk
> except when he rolls in muck
> and STINKS!
> but he just smiles and wags his tail.

"Give it back!" roared Croaky. Her skirt flew above her knees as she snatched the paper.

"Sorry if I've touched a nerve, Maud, your secret is safe with me," said Spike Feet. "I think it's wonderful how well you've bonded with Jasper." She gestured towards the fence. "But your garden's so messy you might have lost your poem. I'd offer my flat for our cake bakes, but…"

Croaky slapped the paper on the table and slammed the tray on top. "You know I can't manage your steep stairs."

I heard a giggle. "Besides, I wanted to see *Fort Knox*."

The women started prodding the food. **How weird is that? I thought food was to eat, not play with.**

I sat smartly and held up a paw until Croaky tossed me a bun. "No more mind, mustn't spoil you." Her eyes twinkled. "I admit Jasper is such good company — even if he *does* keep me on my toes. I love having him here."

I was licking my lips, hoping for another bun, when I spotted Rat slinking along in the shadows. Pretending I needed a pee, I trotted to the shady corner where Rat was hiding out. I jerked my neck, gesturing towards the food table. "It's all yours if you finish the tunnel."

His nose wrinkled. "Nothing's ever free these days."

"Ok, I'll bring out a feast tonight."

Rat narrowed his eyes. "It'll be like putting up a sign: *Eat Here*. All the neighbourhood cats will pour into the garden and then it's bye-bye beef bourguignon. The Stick has the best food for miles. I've worked hard for my place here and I'm not being undermined by the local riffraff."

"How about some cake?" I said.

"The one oozing with cream, or the deal's off."

I looked at Rat's razor-sharp teeth. "Two slices and you start digging?"

"Three."

There was a sudden screech. "Go away, you *'orrible varmint*!" Croaky slammed her hand on the table and stood up, waving her stick.

"Where is it?" Spike Feet's voice trembled, then she stumbled and knocked a plate of little cakes off the table.

I managed to snatch one in my mouth before Croaky picked up the tray. It sliced over the garden, embedding in a tree trunk. "Missed the blighter. *Drat and Double Drat!*"

Her yells spooked Polly and she raced onto the grass and ran around in circles.

"Come back!" shouted Spike Feet. "You could get bitten." She high-stepped over the cakes and tottered towards Polly.

A jet of water burst out and splattered them. Spike Feet's heels dug into the grass and as she lifted each foot, the spikes sank in again. Her clothes clung skin-tight, and water dripped off her cropped white hair.

She peeled off her jacket and shook it in Croaky's face. "Why didn't you warn me?"

"Sorry, it all happened so fast." Croaky's shoulders bounced up and down. "But you must admit it's funny — you look like a drowned rat."

Spike Feet grabbed her bag, then pulled out an object that flashed in the sunshine. I blinked, then saw she was peering at the reflective thing. Her hair had frozen in tiny spikes. She groaned and clamped it down again.

"Oh dear, she won't like that," said Polly.

I heard Rat chuckling from behind the bin. "Best fun I've had in a long time."

Spike Feet pointed a shaking finger at Croaky. Your garden's *infested*! Get Rent-A-Kill right away!"

"Don't worry, I'll kill the skinny weasel," said Croaky.

"It's a *rat*," said a shaky voice.

"I know that!"

Spike Feet sniffed. "Come along, Pol Dol." She clicked her fingers, but Polly stood there and shook a wonderful spray in Croaky's face. Spike Feet pointed a shaking finger at Croaky. "*You're* like a drowned rat now, Mandeville!" She herded Polly through the gate. "Phone Pest Control or I'm not setting foot inside your garden ever again."

Polly pushed her snout through the struts. "Bandit, I've heard that phrase before — animals go flat on their backs. You've got to get out now!"

12. Poisonous Sweets

A metal box stood beside the grill in the drainage hole where spiders liked hanging out. The smell was intriguing. I pawed at the narrow bars and scratched every nook and cranny, but I couldn't reach the little blue sweets inside. So, I started gnawing. When Croaky came out, I zipped behind the bin and tucked my tail out of sight. I wasn't giving up, because there was something about those sweets... I just had to get them, they smelt so

Whisker-Tingling, Drool-Dribbling-Good!

At last, I managed to gnaw a little hole in one corner. My tongue snaked in and scooped a sweet. Then another. Eating is a strong point of mine, but it can also be a flaw… Two led to three, then five...

A strange fuzzy feeling hung around me all day. The stomach cramps started after tea. The gurgly farts were a bit embarrassing. I usually do my poos on walks, but this time I couldn't wait, and did a big squirty one in the garden. When I'd finished, I swayed from side to side and needed my tail to balance.

I'll lie down for a while, have a little nap…

Sounds swirled, then blurred. My tummy was hurting really bad now. Another sound, louder, insistent. Something was shaking my shoulders, but I couldn't lift my head. I was trudging through deep wet sand. That shaking again. My body was churning, and a horrible taste was in my throat. I lurched and spewed strings of goo. I arched again, unable to cough up most of the gunk.

After that, everything went blank.

It was the Victoria sponge that saved me. That's what I think anyway. It soaked up the stomach ache. Croaky fussed around me for days, tucking me in with a duvet, and sitting by my side. She was kind. I heard voices and someone else prodded me and opened my mouth. I was probably sick.

But one morning, I woke up feeling better. The box and the blue sweets had vanished, but Rat was ferreting in the trash as usual. "Still alive, then?" was his greeting.

A bit of juicy rat would have gone down nicely right

then — my tummy was so empty it was rumbling — except weirdly I wasn't hungry.

"That blue stuff was meant for me, you know," said Rat, whisking his tail in the direction of the drain. His squeaky voice was hurting my ears and I wished he'd slither into the drain and never come back.

I followed his gaze and saw a blue rim around the drain. He nodded. "It's murder, that's what, blue murder. The same stuff got my uncle and two of my cousins, and my mum told me never to even sniff a whiff, or it'd get me too." He raised an eyebrow. "But I guess you never listen to advice."

"No one told me."

"Face it, you're just a Greedy Guts."

"I thought you wanted to be in **THE ESCAPE COMMITTEE**," I said with a snarl.

"I do, but…" He flicked his gaze towards Croaky who was shaking white powder around the flowerbeds. "Don't lick it, you'll be stiff in seconds."

"Oh yeah?" I recognised the sweet flowery smell that Mum used in the cottage.

I trotted up to Croaky and she put a finger to her lips. "Don't tell Snootface that it's talcum powder.

There's no way I'm risking your life again with poison."
She tapped her thighs. "Fancy a walk, Jasper? I need to
stretch my legs."

WALK! I danced around her until she clipped on my
lead.

"Oy, where you off to?" said Rat, diving into the bin.

"I'm escaping. Got this amazing plan."

"What is it?" Rat's voice sounded hollow.

I'll think of something, I told myself. The gate
clicked behind us, but something was scuffling along the
wall, rustling the ivy. The noise followed us all the way
down the hill. When we reached the field, Polly was
there. *Her ears!* I couldn't stop staring — they looked
like Croaky's cupcakes, and her fur had been clipped into
a soft cap on her head.

Spike Feet elbowed Croaky. "Good, eh? Would
Jasper like a Bikini Cut like Polly?"

Polly arched her neck, and a ring of sunlight glowed
on the fringes of her fur. "Do you like my new style,
Bandit?"

"It's…" I didn't want to hurt her feelings so I
grinned, as only dogs can. "It's a work of art." She raised
her head and the ball of fur looked like the sponge Isla

used to wash me with.

ISLA! I need to remember my mission!

I strained forwards. "I've just had a great idea. You know you hate cats?" Fear flashed over Polly: wide eyes, shaking legs and twitching eyebrows. I nudged her. "It's not real. You just need to pretend to chase one."

She blinked. "Excuse me?"

"It's simple. You shoot off and the humans get all fired up and Croaky drops my lead in the fuss." I nudged Polly's haunches. "Are you in?"

She glanced at the bench. Croaky and Spike Feet were sitting close together, whispering behind their hands. Croaky leant forward and pushed up her glasses. "I haven't seen the pesky varmint for days."

I eyeballed Polly, and she trotted forward, then looked back. **Some people can't act for toffee.** Then my hackles rose. Something was slinking through the bushes. There actually *was* a cat. Perfect!

But Polly's fur spiked and she froze. *CAT!*

"What's wrong, Pol-Dol?" called Spike Feet. She stood up and pointed. "Oh no, she must've seen that cat."

Polly was shaking in terror, wrecking my plan. "Wimp! That was my chance to escape."

Before Polly could answer me, I saw another animal in the distance. Clumps of grass flew off its claws as it zoomed closer. It wasn't aiming for the cat; it was heading straight for me. I tugged the lead, desperate to be free. Croaky got the hint and reeled it out to its furthest point, but wouldn't let go.

"That cat must really scare dogs," she said. With a sudden shriek, she grabbed her stick and it flew out of her hands, slicing through the air. *"RAT!"*

Spike Feet screamed even louder than Croaky. "It's an *INFESTATION*, we'll all get *RABIES*!"

The ladies jumped onto the bench and clutched each other. I didn't blame them: Rat was about to claw my face off. Spit slathered my whiskers, but he stopped inches away. I gulped. "W…what do you want?"

His eyes rolled, showing the whites. "What d'you think? Polly wasted her chance, so I'm creating a distraction for you. Scarper!"

I stared at my lead, then Rat ran towards the bench, about to leap up. "Morning ladies!"

"AHHHHH!" Croaky held up her arms and let go of the lead.

At last! I dashed through the bushes, the lead whipping from side to side. My tummy was still a bit wobbly, so it took longer than before to reach the river. **No problem, I can swim now.** Kids were laughing and splashing, and a boy was swinging on a rope.

It looked fun, but I wasn't here to play. I launched into the water, my eyes on the opposite bank. A ball whizzed past, splashing my face and water gunged my ears. I ignored it and kept swimming. The lead was pulling at my neck, getting heavier, and the bank wasn't getting any closer.

Plop! Ping! Plop! Missiles flew over my head. I did a spinning back-paddle. How had Croaky got here so fast? More pinecones showered around me. The boy yelled at Croaky to stop, then he let go of the rope, and splooshed into the water. Wild water shot up, then whooshed down on me and the lead dragged me under. I thrashed about, but I couldn't see, couldn't breathe. Everything was dark.

Then suddenly light.

Arms scooped me against a strong chest. Water swished around us as the boy swam back. And there was Croaky with her stick. "I can't thank you enough for saving my little dog."

"You threw pinecones at him," said the boy, his arm tightening around me.

I cuddled closer. **Don't let her take me, please!**

"I was trying to warn Jasper to turn back because he was struggling," said Croaky. She leant against a tree, clutching her chest. "Please, I love him, he's all I have..."

"You'd better give him back," said a girl. "She lives up the street from us and she's just got that cute puppy."

The boy waded to the bank and I slithered onto the ground.

ESCAPE! The thought didn't just pop into my head, it ROARED. But my legs were aching, and I needed a good old shake.

After that, all the children wanted to stroke me. It's been so long since I had a proper tummy tickle. Let's just say it's **Legs in the air, Happy Time**.

I was still lying on my back when Croaky loomed over me. "Thank goodness you're alright, my lovely. You gave me a right shock; my heart was pounding like a steam train." She picked up my lead. "Come on, dear, let's get you home."

13. Isla's Letter

That evening, Rat was sniffing something disgusting. A grey shrunken teabag had gone mouldy. His eyelids flickered. "Like spying on people, do you?"

"No, it's just…thanks for helping me escape."

"You didn't though, did you? I charged down the field for nothing." Razor teeth snapped at me, then he vanished into the bushes.

"Fine, I don't need you!" I headed across the grass, but the **Whizzy Water** jet flared up. Not again! I rolled off the worst of it, then dripped back to the wheelbarrow. And started to dig. Dirt stuck to my wet fur, and grit ran into my eyes. I arched my back and hit the tunnel wall. I tried a low commando crawl, but earth dragged my ears and clogged my mouth.

It's all my fault. I'm going to die, and I'll never see Isla again. The thought made me struggle harder and I clawed the earth, forcing my way up. I ran across the grass, then stood there, panting.

"STOP RIGHT THERE, JASPER!"

I froze. It was yelling in Croaky's voice but where was she? "You've been digging, haven't you?"

The sound was coming from a little white box on the wall. I crept towards it and sniffed. It called my name and I darted from side to side, careering around in crazy circles. It cawed three times. "Priceless! Wait there, I'm coming down."

The door opened and Croaky gurgled like her voice was in water. "I see you've found the Stick-Up Cam." Her eyes gleamed. "Now I'll be able to see if that dratted rat comes back and I'll scare it off, once and for all." She nodded. "*And* intruders. We're going to have so much fun, aren't we, Jasper?" She held out a towel. "Come and get dry, I don't want you catching cold. How about roast duck tonight, or would you prefer fish?"

FISH! A word I know. Sounds like swishing waves. Despite being cold and wet and miserable, I licked my lips.

Croaky clasped her hands. "When it's warmer, we could have fish and chips at the seaside. Would you like that?"

I didn't understand, but she was talking softly and

that meant no cupboard. I followed her inside, then the doorbell rang. I forced my quivering body to calm down and remember the Rules. **Don't bark. Don't run down the hall. Pick up letters for Croaky.**

Her eyes twinkled. "Good boy." She traced the writing with her finger, then she slumped into a chair. When I nosed the envelope, she stroked my head and sighed. "I wish Joey would write. It's from that girl again, Isla."

ISLA! She just said Isla! I sat bolt upright, ears pricked.

The paper flapped. "Alright, hold your horses," said Croaky. "I know how much you like me reading to you."

Dear Bandit,

    I can't believe it's been four weeks since we got here! We've been to the beach loads and it's ok, but not as nice as Cornwall. I want to come home, but Dad's job is a whole year. Another eleven months until I can see you. I hope you liked my poem. My new teacher made me read it to the whole class but I wrote it for you, not them.

Croaky stopped talking but something inside me was jumping. I'd heard Isla's name. She hadn't forgotten me.

It was a strange day. I kept being shooed outside, then Croaky's voice would start cawing louder than the crows who hung around the trees. And the **Whizzy Water** kept firing. I never knew when. Or why.

After dinner, I lay by the fire to dry while Croaky watched TV. "What a load of trash! Why can't there be a good murder?" She dropped the remote on the sofa, then ruffled my ears. "If you'd like a story, I could read one tonight?" I put my head on one side, not understanding, then I glanced at the letter. She pushed up her glasses. "Alright, if I must…"

When we get home, we'll go to the dog-friendly restaurant in Padstow — you know, where the retriever stole your dinner! Do you remember when Harry threw a pasty in the sea near there so the 'dragon' could eat it (the line of rocks that look like spines on a dragon in the water). Then it started to thunder and we ran to the car. And the cottage started to leak, and Mum said it was falling to bits and we had to move.

Croaky tapped her fingers on the letter. "So, the house is falling to bits, is it?" She looked at me over the top of her glasses. "I wonder if that means they'll stay abroad longer than a year? It's so lovely having you around the house." Her eyes were soft and dreamy as she gazed at me. Then she tapped her thighs twice. "Come here, then."

I hesitated, but she was smiling, so I climbed onto her lap. She cuddled me with one arm and it felt nice. Not as comfy and cosy as Isla, of course, but nice.

Then she kept reading.

> Dad always goes on about the words on that stone he found near 'the dragon.' He says it's history and we shouldn't forget. About soldiers who can't grow old because they're dead. I don't know why I'm telling you because you won't understand! But I like the bit about the sun going down and rising in the morning, because I remember you every night when I look at my profile photo.

Croaky slid the letter onto the little table and another

bit of paper wafted onto the floor. I jumped down and retrieved it. I laid the paper on her thighs and gazed at her. She sighed, then her voice bobbed up and down and sounded more choky than usual as she read.

> My dog loves running on the beach
> he races me and always wins and
> spins back swishing sand with his tail
> Teasing me.
>
> He tugs the lead for me to follow
> he's my best friend forever
> I'd follow him anywhere I would
> but they won't let me.

Her lips trembled and stringy mucus hung from her nose, but she didn't swipe it away like normal. She held my head. "You're safe with me, poppet, I've got the security cam now."

14. The Daring Plan

Work on the tunnel was slow. Venturing into the tube made my fur stand on end, but as I couldn't jump over the gate or squeeze underneath, I had to face my fears. Rat said I'd dug deep enough now, and I was on the straight bit under the fence, so I kept clawing into the dark. I tried not to think of how deep I was. Or of the earth piling on top of me and suffocating.

Don't think, just dig. You'll meet Rat's tunnel soon. See Isla again.

But I hit rock. However hard I scratched, it wouldn't cave in. Trembling with exhaustion, I began my slow crawl back. And flopped onto Rat's droppings. That didn't exactly help my mood. Using my secret base as a toilet was bad enough, but I wasn't even sure if Rat was sticking to his side of the bargain.

I trudged across the grass when *WHAM!* I was soaked. I raced around in **grizzly zigzags**, tearing up the grass. I was furious at Rat and sick of dodging the water jets. I couldn't dig if my fur was wet, so the **Whizzy Water** had to go. But whenever I got close, Croaky's voice shouted. It was like she could see me from inside, even with the doors and curtains closed. I needed a friend — let's face it, who'd want to be stuck with Rat and Croaky for company?

That night huge rats peed poison over my dreams. I was flat out when Croaky woke me. "Get up, lazy bones, you're like Joey, sleeping past noon." I tucked my snout under my paw, but she ruffled my fur. "I'm upgrading you into Joey's old room as you're housetrained now."

Baking smells were wafting around. Cake meant Polly would be here soon. So why was Croaky going upstairs? She held onto the bannister and looked over her shoulder. "Come along, Jasper." So I followed her wobbly bottom. There was a strong odour of dead crabs here, but she didn't seem to notice. Why can't humans do their business outside, it would be far easier and the smells would drift away in the air.

She twisted a doorknob at the end of the corridor. "You're at the back of the house. My room's the other side of the landing with a view of Bodmin Moor." She ushered me into a musty room. "Joey was a scruffian and always left smelly socks on the floor." She sighed. "But you're here now." She held a bundle of doggy coats. "Do you fancy the purple, or the orange and black stripes?"

I nosed a random thing.

"No, you can't wear a summer jacket now, dear, the autumn days are drawing in." She lifted something crackly. "How about this sparkly waterproof?"

Something slid something over my head and a strap was attached under my chest. I wriggled as it was itchy. What I really wanted was my bandana. **I might be a sparkly Jasper on the outside, but inside, I was still Bandit with a Bandana who ran free.**

When she didn't take off the jacket, I lifted my paw, trying to get her to understand. Then I rested my head on her knee and gazed into her eyes.

Croaky smiled at me and rubbed my chest. "You look the bee's knees, but I should've bought a bigger size." She unstrapped the jacket, then her hands flowed over my ears in gentle waves. "You used to run everywhere, and your bark could wake the dead...but look at you now. You brighten my days, you really do."

I liked it when she spoke softly. Then her voice popped, and she slid off the bed. "Look lively and let them in, I won't be a mo. I've got a surprise for the old trout."

At the front door I could hear snuffling. **Polly!** I leapt onto a kitchen chair, then stood on two paws to reach the handle.

The door opened and flowery perfume invaded the room. Spike Feet drummed her nails on the worktop. "I've made a perfect chocolate layer cake and she's not even here. Come along, Pol-Dol."

I followed Polly up the path. She was limping. "What's wrong with your leg?"

"It's fine, just aches a bit. I twisted it when I was training for a Show. Must be getting old."

I rubbed my nose against her flank. "You're beautiful."

Polly wagged her tail. "I've missed you, too."

There was a piercing whistle.

"STOP RIGHT THERE, CELIA TROUT!"

The spikes dug into the gravel. "Who's there?"

"The STAR BAKER of Port Isaac!"

Spike Feet jutted out her chin and strutted to the white box on the wall. "I'll *Star Baker* you, Cruella!"

A moment later, Croaky burst out of the Glass

Room, excitement sparking from her. "I got you, didn't I!"

Spike Feet's red lips shrank into a dot. "Face it, Mandeville, you're obsessed."

Croaky arched her neck. "No, the security cam motion detector and water cannon have given me a new lease of life."

"So, what's next: *The Thames Barrier*?" Spike Feet followed Croaky inside and whipped off a flappy coat. "It was bitter bugs out there, waiting for you. I hope it hasn't spoiled my chocolate cake."

"It looks wonderful," said Croaky. "I can't wait to have a slice."

Spike Feet lifted her thin arched eyebrows. "Well, that's a turn-up for the books: you complimenting me."

Croaky cawed. "I guess I must be losing it, in my old age." She grinned at Spike Feet, then stretched down to ruffle my fur. "To be honest, I owe it all to Jasper. I love having him around." She clicked her fingers. "Sit at the table, Jasper."

I jumped onto my chair and heard Polly laughing. A dog's laugh isn't audible to a human, so all they saw was Polly's tongue hanging out in a big smile.

When I looked up again, Spike Feet was pointing at me, and her mouth was hanging open. "But a dog shouldn't…t'int proper."

Croaky ruffled my fur. "Jasper's a marvel. He's learned so many tricks already. All the children down the playpark love him and I'm right proud of him. It reminds me of when Joey lived here, and he'd kick a ball around in the field." A cloud of icing sugar blew over the table when she sighed. I licked my lips, but Croaky didn't notice. She didn't even look up until Spike Feet leant over the table.

"Do you remember when my Rosemary was always over yours when Joe lived with you that summer?"

"The best three months of my life," Croaky said in a soft voice. "I promised his dear mother I'd look after Joey when Martha fell ill during his important exams…" She sighed. "But I had such a grand time with Joey, it almost felt like…"

"He was yours?"

Croaky got up and put her arms around me and I snuggled closer. She might fire up like flames at times, but right now I could sense her need — and let's face it, everyone needs a cuddle.

Croaky guzzled cake all afternoon and her face was smeary, but at last, she let me outside. I crept up to the white box and lifted a paw. When it didn't speak, I snatched it in my teeth and ran towards the fence. I was planning to hide the **Talky Thing** in the tunnel, but when I ducked under the wheelbarrow, Rat was rather busy and his droppings were steaming up my hiding place.

"Oy! Can't a guy get any privacy?" He faced me, ears pricked back, and whiskers sprayed out wider than his body, little front paws on the ground. Then he glanced at the box. "Is that The Stick's new weapon?"

I raised an eyebrow in reply.

He grinned. "Are you thinking what I'm thinking?"

I wagged my tail and dropped the **Talky Thing** down the hole. *Plop!*

It wasn't long before there was a strange, muffled sound. "I can't see anything…blast! The wretched thing's stopped working."

Rat's eyes twinkled. "We've killed it."

My tail lifted. "Right, now to tunnel out."

His nose wrinkled. "Slight hitch…my end's not

quite ready."

"What? I started digging weeks ago. Our tunnels should've joined up by now." I fetched the bucket from the bushes and thrust the hose in Rat's face. "*Do something for once!*" I burrowed to the kink in the tunnel where I found the little box. I felt like giving it a soaking, but you couldn't lift your leg in there, let alone pee. Instead, I clawed soil in the bucket and tugged the hose.

Nothing happened. I tugged harder and it rocked against me. Rat was pulling his weight at last. The hose was alive, snaking from side to side, then the bucket shot up the tunnel. **Surely Rat can't pull that hard?**

As I wriggled out, I smelt cheesy feet. To my horror, I came face to face with Croaky! She swung the bucket above my head and my body tensed. Could I scramble away in time, or should I dive down again?

But she didn't throw the bucket at me, she placed it gently on the ground. Her voice was soft, questioning. Perhaps she hadn't realised what I was up to?

She lifted me up and rubbed the earth off my snout. "I don't understand. Why would you do this? Here's me thinking all the time you were the rat catcher, but instead, you're the rat." She stroked my ears. 'I thought we were happy together, I cook you nice meals and I care for you, don't I?" Her glasses went all misty, I think her eyes were leaking.

I put my head on one side, wondering what she wanted and what I should do.

Her lower lip wobbled and her voice cracked into bits. "I love you Jasper. I'd do anything for you, I couldn't bear it if you weren't around." She removed her glasses and wiped her eyes. Sadness swirled into me.

Then suddenly, hot anger. Her arms swished like Rat's tail when he's angry. The atmosphere had turned dangerous. I fled to the bushes and lay trembling.

A massive THUD. I peeped out. The wheelbarrow had landed on a bush; bits were spiking up either side like a bad hairstyle. Croaky was going wild: slashing and swiping, uprooting and destroying. Splinters and leaves were flying everywhere. Water bubbled on her forehead, and I'd never smelt sweat this bad. When she stopped, there was a great hollow where the tunnel had been and a mountain of rubble.

A whole month's work gone in a single evening.

15. He's My Dog!

As the weeks went by, the weather grew wetter and soggy earth squished under my paws. Cold winds picked up rubbish and lifted skirts and umbrellas into the air. Hats flew across the field, tumbling in front of laughing children. Trees shivered and lost their leaves. I felt lonely, too. Rat had scarpered and Polly hadn't come over for ages. And the earth was rock solid, impossible to dig.

That morning, Croaky and I were outside; she was rubbing her arms and blowing clouds in the air. "Come inside Jasper, it's freezing. I've got chills up my pantaloons."

I backed away and flicked my gaze to the gate. She leant forward, reaching for my collar. "Oo-err, it's a bit *ic…eeee!"* She hopped then skidded then crashed. *"Ooo, me Blooming Bum!"* She clutched her backside with both hands. "That's it, we're stopping in all winter."

My life fell into a routine of food, training and sleep. I tried my best to escape, but whenever the doorbell rang (which was rare), Croaky shut me in the kitchen. She spent every evening in the Fire Room watching TV. I often leant against her legs, asking to be let out, but when humans are watching the screen, they don't see me.

Months passed with hard ground underfoot, then at last, there was change in the air and I sniffed new life. Sparrows and bluetits combed the patio each morning, collecting beakfuls of stray hairs. I kept my distance in case they swooped down and pulled off the rest of my fur. Flowers poked up and little bugs were busy.

The only thing that wasn't active was **THE ESCAPE COMMITTEE**. Rat popped his head up at daybreak or dusk, but he had his paw in other pies, and Polly was always busy preparing for some dog show. I was glad when the weekly bake-offs started up again and I saw Polly when she brought Spike Feet over, but I rarely saw her down the field.

But every day there were new things to investigate and curls of excitement in the air. The garden was bursting with scent. I loved the buzz of insects, and I had fun running at the blackbirds with wriggly worms in their beaks. The sun woke me earlier, warming my fur; and as the weather grew hotter, the playpark was bouncing with children and there were lovely licky drips of ice cream. I'd pull the lead towards the squeals of laughter. But it was never Isla.

Then one day, an envelope popped onto the mat. When Croaky opened it, her neck went from side to side. Then she stopped and her chest heaved. Then she folded like a flower at night: her back curved and her forearms rested on her knees, crumpling the letter. She was staring at her hands, her breath shuddering.

"I knew this day would come, but I'd be so lost without you, Jasper, so lonely." Her lower lip wobbled and her glasses steamed up. "I'd never leave you like they did, just go away like that. It's cruel, that's what it is, downright cruel. You're *my* dog now, aren't you, poppet?" She took off her glasses and sniffed. "*And* Isla keeps calling you the wrong name: you aren't a bandit, you're a Lady's Companion. It took a year to train you, but you're obedient now."

Isla! I wagged my tail when I heard the beloved name. **Was I going to see Isla again soon?**

Croaky stroked my chin and rubbed my chest. "You're happy here, aren't you Jasper? You'd prefer to stay with me, wouldn't you, lovey?"

She tore up the letter, but its sweet scent clung to me all day. I watched shadows cross the curtains and that night I dreamed I was running on the beach. When I woke up, the longing was so intense that I could almost smell the salty seaweed and hear the splash of the waves.

I don't remember which day it was — everything jumbled into crazy circles after the letter came — but I remember I was licking my lips after a juicy beef steak when I heard a voice that made my muscles tingle. Footsteps crunched the gravel. Another voice, a young boy. A joyful bark jumped all over me. The doorbell rang and I scrambled off my chair, but Croaky sped like a greyhound and got there first.

A whiff of paint. A man was standing on the doorstep. My tail whipped from side to side. **Dad!**

"Joey," Croaky sounded all light and bubbly. "How lovely to see you. I've got the money."

Dad shook his head. "I told you he's not for sale."

Then a familiar sweet scent swam around me. I was alive with longing and joyful whimpers raced around my throat.

"I can hear Bandit!"

ISLA! That's my Isla who runs like the wind!

My whiskers were twitching, my nostrils were sniffing and everything inside me was buzzing with excitement. I barked and squeezed past, but Croaky pulled me back. "I explained on the phone. I need him, he's given me a new lease of life."

"I know you did," said Dad, "and that's wonderful, but he's still not yours."

Why wasn't Croaky opening the door? I needed to get out and be with my family.

Dad was speaking again, and I sensed a cloud of anxiety around him. "I told you we were coming to fetch him today."

"And I wrote a letter." I made happy jumpy noises when I heard Isla again, and my tail whacked Croaky's thigh. Her legs split, blocking me.

"Bandit!" called Isla. "I can see Bandit!"

Isla's voice leapt into me, and I ran around in circles, barking. **My family has come for me at last!**

I nipped under Croaky's skirt and bounded closer, trying to lick Isla's hand. But Croaky slid the chain across the door. "I'm sorry, then you've had a wasted journey."

Her voice had gone flat.

When I nosed my snout through the crack, she snapped at me. "Get back, Jasper."

"Jasper, who's Jasper?" Mum's voice.

The letterbox flipped open, and Isla's eyes locked onto mine. Her fingertips reached through and stroked my muzzle. "Bandit, I've missed you so much.

Isla, I love you!

My tail thumped the door, but Croaky barged it shut with her bum. "Go away, he's mine now."

"He's not *your* dog, he's *ours!*"

Isla's angry words cut into me. She was right behind the door. Why wouldn't it open? I needed to get to her, she was hurting. I darted from side to side, barking, but Croaky yanked my neck. "Shut up!"

"Don't you tell my daughter to shut up," said Dad.

"No, that was…" Croaky coughed. "Just talking to myself." She opened the door a crack again, then put her arms around me. "Jasper's been a godsend. I've paid for all his clothes and we go to Pamper Parlour every fortnight…he's my dog now."

"HE'S NOT YOUR JASPER, HE'S OUR BANDIT!" I went frantic when I heard the pain in Isla's voice, and I whimpered and strained to get free. When Croaky didn't let me go, Isla's voice slammed into the door.

"GIVE HIM BACK!"

Mum was speaking in a soft, calm tone, but when I heard Isla crying, my whimper turned into a howl.

"I'm sorry, I really am," said Croaky, "but I'm old and I need a dog for security."

"Looks like you've already got that with the high fence and the security cams," said Dad. "Bandit tried to escape, didn't he?"

The door banged shut again. Croaky stood there, her hands shaking. But I could still hear Isla shouting. And smell her scent. I ran to the Fire Room and jumped on the armchair, my paws on the windowsill. When I saw Isla, my nails tore at the glass. **I'm here, I'm here!**

Isla raced towards me and spread her palms on the window. Her lips were wobbling and her eyes were leaking. I whimpered and ran to the door and back to the window, desperate to get out.

Tappity-tap. The sound was getting louder. Right behind me. *Tappity tap. Tap...*

I felt the fear of the cupboard and spun around,

quivering. Croaky jabbed her stick at the window. "Go away and leave us alone!"

Isla shouted and banged the glass. They faced each other like two dogs in attack mode. Croaky's glasses slipped down her nose and clattered on the floor, but she didn't pick them up. Then Mum pulled Isla's arm down. I yelped, but their faces were going all misty.

Croaky lurched towards me and her fingers stroked my chin. "It's alright Jasper, I love you, too. We're the *Dream Team*, aren't we, poppet?" The movements were soft and gentle so I stood as still as I could until I could get to Isla. But the pressure grew firmer, and my collar grew tighter until my throat hurt. A growl rumbled in my chest and shot into my throat. The window banged again and someone screamed.

And suddenly I was free. Croaky was staring straight ahead, frozen. Then she clutched her chest and there was a loud crash. Her body was sprawled on the floor. Her hair all scrawly. Her hands not moving. Like a dead bird fallen from the sky.

The banging stopped. Mum cupped her hand over her mouth and Isla's cheeks squished against the window. Worry dug inside me. I glanced at Croaky and nosed her face. She held onto a chair arm and slowly stood up, then hobbled over to the window. The curtains swished, blocking my family.

More shouting. The doorbell kept ringing. I ran into the hall and clawed the door. **Get me out of here!**

Croaky barged past, blotting my view. Then she stumbled. "Oy, there's no need to poke me."

The letterbox had flipped open again. "Are you alright Maud? Shall we call an ambulance?" Mum.

Croaky spun around. "It was the shock...Jasper's such a good companion and what with my dodgy heart..." She clutched her chest. "Please leave us alone."

Whispers. Footsteps.

My whimper turned into a bark. **No, don't go!**

Isla started to cry. Then Dad's eyes looked at me through the letterbox. "Please Maud. My daughter's so upset — we all are. You can easily buy your own dog. Or go to a dog shelter? Didn't you have a rescue dog before?"

Croaky squatted, facing the letterbox. "But I love him and he's such a comfort to an old woman with no family. Surely, it's the least you can do, Joey, when I looked after you when your poor mother was in hospital."

She cleared her throat, then spoke more loudly. "Then I took you in again when your father fell off that ladder and broke his back so soon after the funeral."

"Stop trying to guilt-trip me!" Spray flew onto my whiskers as words shot back through the gap; Dad had his hackles up.

"But I'm not the one who caused the accident, am I?" said Croaky. "I've kept my silence all these years. Do you want me to tell your family exactly what happened?"

Dad sucked in a deep breath, then his face came closer and I saw fear in his eyes. "You wouldn't—" he whispered.

"Not if you let me keep Jasper," said Croaky in a low voice. She held my collar. "Look, I'll buy you another dog if you like, but he's *my* dog now."

Dad shot out of view. Mum and Isla were talking to Dad, they sounded worried and jittery.

Silence. But the silence was full of stress. A dark cloud was pressing in on me from all sides. Unhappiness. Anger. Fear. I kept whining so my family would know I was on their side, that I understood, even if I didn't.

Don't be sad. Come and get me. I'll make you happy again, I promise.

Dad crouched down again and his forehead was a mass of lines. His voice got squeaky, pleading. "But we had an agreement, we said a year."

Anxiety was flooding into me, swamping me. I whimpered, trying to get close to Dad and his eyes started to leak. I reached forward to lick his face, but Croaky pulled me back. "Where is it, in writing? Where's the proof? Huh?"

"But we *trusted* you, you *promised*."

16. Facing the Monster

The doorbell kept ringing the next morning, but Croaky kept stirring the porridge. She stirred so hard that bits dolloped on the floor. I skidded in for a flying lick, then ran down the corridor. Why wasn't she opening the door? I darted upstairs and jumped on my big bed, resting my paws on the windowsill. The voices were fainter here; I needed to be at the front.

Croaky's bedroom? I glanced across the corridor and my paw hovered in mid-air. **It's forbidden…she'd go ballistic…but she's keeping me prisoner…**

Something broke inside me and I nosed the door. The crabby scent throbbed in my throat, but I could hear Isla's voice and I *had* to see her. Her wonderful sweet scent was pouring through the open window, blocking out the stuffy room. The bed wasn't beside the window like mine, so I scrambled onto a chair, then stood on a shiny table. I lifted my snout and breathed in my family. They were on the path; I could see their heads. My tail whacked the air and a white tissue fluttered off the table. I was desperate to let rip, but if Croaky heard me she'd be onto me in seconds. So, I made snuffly little whimpers and excited whines, hoping they'd look up.

Mum flapped her hands and said something to Isla, who disappeared. I heard the smack of a window being tapped hard. Isla reappeared and tugged Dad's arm. "*Do* something! I can't believe you lived here with *her*!"

More talking. Then a swish, a ping, something hitting the wall. "You always say that. It's not fair!" Isla's hair flew around her shoulders as she was pulled towards the gate.

A bark stormed into my throat, tearing me to pieces.

Come back! Don't leave me!

I kept barking when the car drove away. They didn't hear me.

But someone else did. "How *dare* you come into my room!" Croaky's words crunched like gravel as she stamped towards me.

My legs trembled. I took a quick glance at the window. Croaky snarled and raised her stick. I eyed the floor. A standing jump isn't easy off a slippery table, but when you're about to be whacked, you've no choice. I skidded, then spun around to face the monster.

She ran her finger over the shiny table and her lip curled. "You've ruined my dressing table! Just look at those scratches you've made." A storm of anger shook her body and her eyes almost popped out of her glasses.

Something bad was going to happen if I didn't get out right now.

I bolted for the door, but Croaky crouched with wide arms, blocking the exit. She bared her teeth. I dodged, snapping back in fear.

"STOP BARKING!" she screamed. "WE DO NOT SHOUT! WE ARE POLITE!" Her glasses flashed and she herded me into the corner. I whisked my tail before it was trampled. There was nothing for it but to bomb under her skirt.

Croaky squeezed her legs together. I was trapped. And it smelt worse than ever. I headbutted her leg and it kneed me. I squealed and nipped the skirt in my teeth.

Let me out!

The curtain lifted, but she grabbed the scruff of my neck. And dragged me across the room and down the stairs. *Bump, bump, bump.*

But she didn't go to the cupboard. She strode to the

Fire Room where she put me down. Then she opened a drawer in the cabinet. Something jingled in her hand. My nostrils quivered.

Hey, that's mine! I sat up straight, my gaze flicking to the tag and back to Croaky.

I lifted a paw. **Please...pretty please...?**

Her lips twisted and she threw the tag in the air. I leapt but she caught it in one hand.

Oh, so this is a game?

As her elbow moved back, my legs tensed, ready to spring and catch the tag. But she grasped it in her fist. "Say goodbye because that's the last you'll see of it." She stormed upstairs and I heard the toilet flush. The stairs creaked and a shadow loomed over me. "Now there's no proof." She swooped lower and swung me against her chest, my legs paddling the air.

As the corridor flashed past, I felt a growing dread. The cupboard door swung open, and I landed in a heap. "This is your home, and don't you forget it. They're never getting you back, you're mine."

17. Croaky's Story

They may have come back, but I didn't know because the cupboard was my new home that day. And the next.

On the third day, Croaky didn't lock me away again after my morning pee. "How about a full English breakfast with a squirt of tomato sauce?" she said in a happy voice. "And I've got some fish in, your favourite; I thought we could have baked lemon sole tonight."

My plate was piled high with sausages, bacon, baked beans, mushrooms and fried egg. I guess it was Croaky's way of saying sorry. I was glad she was in a good mood again, but my plan was to gulp everything down then get out of here. And it was a stonker of a breakfast today, a

Licky-Likey-Scrum-Doodle!

Croaky smiled. "No hard feelings, eh?" I stared at her, then flicked my gaze to the door. She got the hint.

High-pitched buzzing was above me, but I ignored it and itched a spot that was getting to me. If my paw whirred even faster, it might catapult me over the horrible fence.

"Give over, you're making me dizzy." Rat was back. He was sitting on the fence, swinging his tail.

"But I have to find my family. She locked me away all week!"

"She's a right whacko." Rat lifted his head. "I bet that huge buzzy wasp is another of her schemes."

I looked up and saw a massive black wasp-bird flying circles above us.

"Oy, watch out, it's THE STICK!" yelled Rat.

But Croaky wasn't looking at us, she was shaking her fist at the sky. "Wretched drones. Shouldn't be allowed." She clutched her chest, then went back into the house.

A few minutes later, an upstairs curtain caught my attention. "Jasper? Come and look at my zip wire, it's the bee's knees."

I walked a few paces and looked up.

"A bit closer…" She touched something on her windowsill, and it flew towards me then jerked back.

Bluuurrrr! A bucket of water tipped over my head. I shook an angry arc of water over the garden. Croaky cheered. "It works! Mandeville, you've excelled yourself."

I was rolling on the grass when she swooped in with a towel and patted me. "If they come back, they'll get a right soaking."

She took me inside, then two envelopes fell on the doormat. Her lips squished as her finger ran along a page and she started chewing her cheek — she should've had a bigger breakfast. "I'm sick to death of them pestering us. Why won't they accept that you're mine now?" The sofa sank and she held out her arms. "Come here Jasper. I'm sorry I got cross. I didn't want to lock you in that cupboard, you know, it was for your own safety."

I wriggled free and pawed a flappy corner of the letter. She flicked it and stared at where it had fallen. Then, with a sudden whoosh of breath, she leapt in the air, her skirts flapping. Energy was sparking off her, hot and sticky.

She grabbed her phone. "WHY...DID...YOUR... DAD...BREAK...HIS...BACK?" she said as she tapped. She nodded at me. "That should do the trick. If Joey thinks I was joking about revealing the truth about his dad's accident, he's got another thing coming. Joey used to talk in his sleep, you know. You should never have secrets if you talk in your sleep."

I backed away and sniffed the other envelope.

"Oh, give it here, then." Croaky ripped it open and her neck moved from side to side. "At least she's got my name right at last…"

Please give my dog back! Mum bought Bandit as a puppy for my birthday. It's not fair you keeping him because he's OURS! And he loves us, I know he does. What if you were taken away and forced to stay somewhere you didn't want to be, you'd hate it too, wouldn't you?

Croaky's back curved and her shoulders sagged. *"Forced to stay somewhere you didn't want to be…"* Her voice sounded different, far away. Her chin got lower until it touched her chest and trembly breaths shook her body. "But she couldn't know that Daddy used to lock me in my room…no one knew, only Mummy."

I sensed darkness inside her and began to whine. She murmured something and stroked my ears, then her nails suddenly clamped on my head. "He said I was naughty, and I needed to be taught a lesson…and it hurt, it always hurt…"

Harsh croaky breathing. My head was spinning, stinging. I whimpered and twisted, but her stringy snot dripped on my muzzle. "One day, Mummy was gone, and I was stuck with *him*. You wouldn't ever leave me, would you, Jasper?" She leant closer, her musky scent overpowering me. "I couldn't cope without you now."

It was worse than being trapped in the tunnel. Then the pressure released, and she twirled the end of my ear around her fingers.

I edged away, afraid she'd switch back into a monster. But she stood up and clasped her hands. "Now then, a card popped through the door yesterday with an offer to fit a security alarm. Where did that get to?" She nodded. "We need to keep intruders out, don't we?" She leant towards me "And keep *you* in."

18. Slimebug Slinks In

Another week passed, but I didn't see Isla. My ears pricked up when every car drove past, but my family never came back. Just a tall man with long spidery legs. His trousers had the scent of a dog, an old dog in pain. The man had a thin pinched face and a sharp pointed nose. When he saw me, his eyelids flickered and his nostrils twitched. He crept along beside the wall, sliding his feet. **Oozing like a slimy slug.**

Croaky pulled a creased tissue out of her waistband and offered it. The man shook his head. "It's my asthma; the dog hairs…" He reached for a little tube and sniffed it. Then he took a pencil out of his brown suit pocket. "I'll install the burglar alarm here, next to the door."

I approached, tail erect, and he edged away, looking at me over his shoulder. "It doesn't bite, does it?"

Croaky pressed her hand on her chest. "Of course not, Jasper's highly trained."

There was something about the man I didn't trust.

His movements were slow, but I sensed he could suddenly lash out and sting. "Just checking, madam, you can't be too careful." Slimebug wiped his hand across his nose. "It's *your* security I'm concerned about. You never know who's prowling around." He glanced at his fingers, then rubbed them down his trousers. "Especially on these dark nights now summer's almost over."

I backed away from his shiny pointed shoes, but Croaky leant towards him. "I'm sorry I can't offer a coffee; I've got an appointment at the Pamper Parlour."

A smell of rotten eggs poured into my nostrils as Slimebug breathed out. "You don't need pampering, you're beautiful as it is."

"Oh, do you really think so?" Croaky's voice went all gurgly like it was stuck in water.

Slimebug smothered a cough under his hand. "I'll be back with the goods later, say four o'clock?"

When he'd gone, Croaky tugged her hair into a tight bun, then she pulled bits down around her ears. Nervous excitement was buzzing around and she couldn't sit still. I knew what she needed, so I sat beside the cupboard door where she kept the lead. She got the hint.

We met Polly and Spike Feet down the field.

Croaky's gaze kept flitting about and her words were hopping all over the place. "'Ere, have you heard that wretched drone? They'd better not come near my house again, because I'm buying a top-of-the-range security alarm."

Spike Feet's nose looked bigger as she glanced down. "What company's fitting it?"

"Mr Brown."

"Not *Smith*?" Spike Feet raised an eyebrow. "Well don't say I haven't warned you about scam artists."

While our humans chatted, I told Polly about my family turning up. "I have to leave as soon as I can, before winter sets in."

Her tail drooped. "I'll miss you."

"Come with me. You could live at the cottage."

"I have my own human."

"It'll be fine; they love dogs." I remembered Harry using my ears as aeroplane wings, but I had a rush of love when I thought of Isla. "Please Polly?"

Polly winked. "Ok, next time we're over at your place, I'll help you escape."

Excitement that I might see Isla at last, made me pant. "I'd be on my best behaviour, so I'm not locked in the cupboard."

"The cupboard?"

"When she punishes me, she locks me in there."

"That's horrible." Polly touched noses. "Why didn't you tell me before?"

I glanced at my paws. "I don't know…what could you do?"

"Be here for you. We're friends, aren't we? That's what friends do."

I felt choked up and let Polly lick my face. And a memory flashed into my mind of another dog doing this when there were lots of puppies tumbling around, but it was so long ago I couldn't remember their faces.

A white van was waiting outside Croaky's house, and a smell of rotten eggs was hovering around. We'd only just closed the door when the bell rang.

Slimebug stood there with another man. Croaky smiled. "How lovely to see you, Mr...?" Her eyebrows jammed together, and she chewed her cheek.

Slimebug snaked out a long thin arm to shake her hand. "Brown." He tipped his head to his companion, a man with a round face and several chins. "And this is Mr Smith."

The other man touched his flat cap. "Afternoon, missus." He crouched down and stroked me. "Cute dog. What's 'ee called?"

"Jasper."

Flatcap patted me and one of the dungaree straps slipped off his shoulder. It flapped loose as he stood up.

Slimebug pressed his back against the wall and sucked up a lungful of snot. He glared at me. "Call your dog off, will you?"

"It's fine, Jasper's just saying hello."

His lips twisted in a snarl. "Growling means hello… I'll have to remember that." He stepped inside. "May I?"

Croaky's neck stretched. "But I said four."

"What a memory you have, madam!" Slimebug's tongue flicked to the corner of his mouth and he flapped a leaflet. "It's the very latest super sensitive alarm, highly effective. The sooner we get it in, the better." He edged Croaky into the house.

I watched on high alert. Darkness was all around Slimebug and she couldn't see it. Why was she offering him a biscuit? She should get rid of him.

"Right boss, where d'yer want it?" said Flatcap.

After he'd fitted the box on the wall, Flatcap's hands hung down as if he didn't know where to put them. The box had a button that glowed. Slimebug seemed to glow, too; I didn't like the energy fizzing around him.

Fiery. Hot. Dangerous.

He thrust some paper into Croaky's hand, and her jaw dropped open.

"You're paying for the best," said Flatcap.

"You're right there, Smithers," said Slimebug. He leant towards Croaky, clasping his hands. "But just for you, Maud — may I call you Maud — I'll offer a special deal."

"I do like a bargain. I'll just make a cuppa."

When Croaky disappeared, Slimebug clutched Flatcap's shirt, pulling him closer. "Did you switch it off?"

"Wot?"

Slimebug cuffed Flatcap on the head. "My drone, idiot. I've got some awesome aerial photos."

I was guarding the door, waiting for Croaky, but Slimebug stuck out his tongue. "Stop staring, mutt."

"Shush Boss, the old bat's coming," said Flatcap.

Croaky brought in a wobbly tray of drinks. "It's

lovely to have visitors. Shall we sit in the conservatory?”

“Yeah, let’s take a gander,” said Slimebug.

The men slurped their tea, then roared off in the van. Croaky smoothed her hand along the alarm box, then she picked up her phone. “I can’t wait to tell Celia I got it half price.”

The voice on the other end sounded angry. Croaky stamped her foot. “No, I was *not* conned. Jasper was here, and he heard everything.”

I heard my name and wagged my tail, and Croaky waved at me. “Shush, Jasper, Mummy’s on the phone. Sorry Celia, what was that?” She glared at the phone. “How could you *say* that? He means *everything* to me.”

The voice bubbled up again, and Croaky slammed the phone down. “Insufferable woman.” She held my head with both hands and gazed at me. “You’re my little saviour, Jasper. You always listen. I was going to tell Celia about my heart murmur but now I shan’t.”

Her eyes leaked onto my fur, then she sniffed and smoothed them away. “Well, no one’s going to steal you now I’ve got my alarm.”

19. Polly Tries to Help

I lay on my belly and watched feet walk past, but it was never Isla. In desperation, I cannoned into the gate, but it wouldn't budge, and the scratchy wire was still curled around the top. If only I was taller like Polly, I might be able to jump it. She was easy to spot with her curly topknot, but whenever I saw her in the distance, Croaky pulled me back. I waited for weeks, but my family never came back. Nor did Polly. I missed her.

Croaky stooped more and her feet dragged along the floor. There were no lovely **Cakey-Bakey** smells, not even a hint of cheese scones. Another letter came today and she dropped it in the bin. I tried to pull it out, but she wagged her finger and said, "No." Then she curled up on the sofa with a book. Her breathing grew slower and the book slipped onto the floor, the pages splayed out. I nosed her arm to alert her, then she reached down.

"You're a little bookworm, aren't you? Right, we've got to where Peter pushed the wheelchair down the mountain." Croaky's voice rose and fell in soft waves, then she began to stutter. "Heidi felt so lost and alone." She shut the book and hugged me. "But I've got you now, haven't I?"

⚬

She read every evening after that. Then one day she started baking again and the table was bursting with cakes and pastries. Polly and Spike Feet arrived and all seemed to be forgiven.

Polly scratched her ear. "The Bikini Cut was a bit severe this time; she'll be devastated if I don't win Best in Show again." Polly had her nose in the air like she was being judged already.

I shook my ears. "You're not doing another Show, you're coming with me, remember?"

Polly flicked an eyelid. "But Spike Feet needs me."

"No! We need to be free."

"Are you sure? You keep talking about finding your Forever Family, but you're still here, aren't you?"

My whiskers twitched and I felt like scratching my hind quarters. "It's not my fault she never lets me off the lead. If she did, I would've been off like a shot."

Polly put her paw over one eye. "If you say so, *Jasper*."

"I am NOT Jasper!"

But I feared that I was becoming more Jasper than Bandit every day. I offered our humans napkins for their crispy cakes, and I only ate when Croaky had finished her mouthful. The days were long gone when I was tempted to take snacks. When a cherry muffin slipped onto the floor, I never even slavered.

It *had* to stop. I reminded Polly she'd offered to help me escape.

She glanced at Spike Feet. "I'll get her to open the gate, then you run for it." She started to pant.

Spike Feet tutted three times. "I thought you did a pee-pee before we left, Polly? You can't go in Maud's garden, you'll have to do your business outside." She got up and swung open the gate, and Polly squatted on the grass verge.

Why am I standing here? Quick, run! I skidded through the gate, heart pounding, before Croaky could stop me. Then I flew down the path.

It happened so fast.

A whoosh of air. A screech of brakes.

A shout. Clickety-click heels.

A scream. High and long. "POLLY!"

The shiny black handbag skidded past me, everything spilling out. I whipped around in panic and ran back. Spike Feet was kneeling on the grass, cradling Polly's head in her lap. "No! My beautiful girl! My beautiful Pol-Dol!" Her eyes were leaking onto Polly's fur.

I nosed Polly. Her eyelids flickered, but didn't open. I licked her face, trying to wake her. "Polly, what's wrong?" She whimpered, but didn't move. She was still breathing. Just.

Croaky leant on the gate and yelled at the motorbike. A man in a helmet was standing up, legs either side of the machine. He held up his arms and walked towards us, but Croaky yelled at him again. He hovered, then retreated. The engine roared past and was gone.

And I feared that Polly had gone too. I howled in despair. When Spike Feet scooped her limp body into her arms, I crept back to the house and cowered in my basket. It was all my fault. If I hadn't run out so wildly, that motorbike wouldn't have swerved into the curb and whooshed Polly. I whimpered in fear. **You're such a**

good friend Polly, I love you. Please be alright.

I lay by the gate the next day. Whenever a dog came past, I jumped up, then my tail drooped and I sank down again, nose on paws. It wasn't just me who was depressed. Croaky leant like a tree in the wind and shuffled along facing the ground taking shallow rapid breaths.

When we reached Polly's house, Croaky hovered on the doorstep and the upstairs curtain twitched. But no one opened the door. Croaky leant on the red box for support and touched her chest. "Dratted palpitations."

She led me to the park bench where she sat, and I sniffed the scrappy grass and sweet wrappers. Dogs always pee near benches and you can find out who's been there. But I couldn't smell Polly's scent.

Then, suddenly, I could.

Spike Feet was walking towards us. But Polly had gone, hadn't she; it must just be her scent clinging to her human.

Then a wild curly topknot appeared behind Spike Feet. It *was* Polly! She had a white bandage around her leg and her foot was hovering off the ground like she didn't want to put it down.

But she was here, she was alive!

I rushed towards her, wagging my tail. "Polly, I thought I'd never see you again."

Her ears pricked and she nosed me, saying hello. "You can't get rid of me that easily. My leg aches a bit, but I'll be fine."

"But the motorbike...?"

Polly grinned. "It's all my Training for the Shows: I'm good at speedy jumps."

I bounced around her, overjoyed. "Now you can come to the cottage by the sea."

Polly's eyebrow lifted as she flicked her gaze at Spike Feet. "I already told you I can't." She looked down at her trembling paw. "Anyway, I couldn't go far with my limpy leg. No, you must go and look for your family. You will never be happy until you find them."

The next day, I hatched a new escape plan. There was a slither of light between two planks in the back fence where Croaky had hurled the wheelbarrow, and it had steadily been getting bigger with every storm. (Ok, so I'd also been gnawing and clawing at it — anything to stop the boredom.)

Sunlight was winking, inviting me to escape. With a massive run-up, I was sure I could burst through. Croaky never went down that end of the garden now, and the wheelbarrow was full of greenish slimy water. The stink reminded me of Slimebug. Rat liked sniffing in it, but hey, everyone knows he's weird. But at least he was onboard with my idea.

We were having our final de-briefing session and energy was bubbling inside me. Rat swished his tail at me. "Sure you've sussed out the layout?"

I arched my neck high above him. "Like the back of my paw, I've been here long enough."

"Alright mate, just saying. What's the plan when you get through the hatch?"

"Get into the kitchen cupboard where she keeps the cake tins, then climb through the little grill." I nodded at Rat. "Which you'll gnaw open."

"No problem." He grinned. "Make sure you run wide of the water jets, then…"

Tunnel to Freedom! My tail did a victory swish and my whiskers tingled with excitement. Everything had been planned perfectly, it was going to happen at last.

I tapped on the door to go inside. And waited until Croaky had gone to bed.

Warm night. Perfect.

Full moon. Not so perfect.

But everything was ready; it was now or never.

I crept out of my bedroom and the floor creaked. A loud snore gave me the **Wibbly-Wobblies** and I began to pant. A hissy fart escaped before I could stop it. If my tummy didn't stop jingling, I'd give myself away.

I tiptoed downstairs and across the hall, then squeezed through the door to the Fire Room which I'd left ajar. Next, I nudged the doors into the Table Room.

Jump onto the sideboard.

Squeeze through the hole into the kitchen.

I couldn't believe how easy it was. I nosed the tall cupboard door, then took a running jump onto the cold worktop. And skidded into some jam jars. One was rolling towards the edge. I shoved it back just in time, but more were wobbling. I leapt up and stood on hind legs. "Rat, I'm here!" I tapped the metal grill and called again.

Still no answering squeak. But the mesh was loose, so he'd done his part. I head-butted the grill and it swung on its hinges and clattered on the path.

A drop of about eight feet. Easy peasy.

Jump clear of that big pot.

I misjudged and landed smack in it. Broken china and flying earth spattered the patio. My eyes blurred. Pain dug into me. I was a mass of prickles.

BOOM! The garden lit up.

I panicked and ran across the grass.

WHOOSH!

I didn't stop to shake off the water, faster and faster I ran, my eyes on the target. Moonlight lit up Rat who was sitting on the wheelbarrow.

"See you've stuck to the plan. It took me ages to gnaw that grill loose and you've goofed it up — let the whole world know you're escaping."

His voice was mocking, but he gestured at the wheelbarrow. "Hurry up, mate!" But I couldn't, not yet. I pretended to itch a burr on my backside so he wouldn't know I was in great pain.

His ears suddenly twitched, and he leapt down.

"Watch out, it's *The Stick*!"

POW! A tin smashed against the fence. White bits pinged back and splattered the flowerbeds.

"Mmm, rice pudding," said Rat. He took a quick lick, then slithered into the darkness.

I wanted to follow, but my legs wouldn't move. Then a heavy thud shook the ground and any hope of escape crumbled.

20. The Insider

My punishment had been watching Croaky nailing more lumps of wood over the cracked fence. She huffed and hammered, she puffed and panted, then the job was done. When we went out, she kept me on a tight lead; I was her walking stick that day. Not that I felt like dashing around because I was still aching after my botched escape.

The pavements grew icy and breath hovered in the cold air. I was stuck in the garden during the long cold months. She insisted on dressing me in thick jackets, even though my fur kept me warm.

One morning, I woke up to wind whistling around the house and rippling the grass. The glass door rattled for hours, and plastic bags flew past the windows. I didn't like it and nor did Croaky. She fidgeted and pulled stray hairs out of her bun like she did when she was worried.

"Jasper, do you remember when you came here? You ate off the floor — a disgusting habit — and I thought I'd made a huge mistake." She chewed her lip. "I did the right thing not giving you back, didn't I? I can't help thinking..."

BANG! The door shivered. A whoosh of cold air. I knew it was Spike Feet before I saw her because a strong smell of flowers wafted over me, and the garden flowers had shrivelled up for winter. I could smell Polly on her clothes, but Polly wasn't here. Spike Feet stamped her big flat boots and swung a carrier bag onto a chair.

"How are you, Maud?"

Croaky folded her arms. "Fine."

"You don't sound fine, Mandeville, I want the truth."

"Just a few palpitations." She touched the left side of her chest. "I'm fine, but what about your Polly?"

"Left her at home. She's still in a cast and I thought the hill would be too much for the poor old girl."

I heard Polly's name and wagged my tail. Then I nosed the bag and some books tumbled out. Spike Feet patted me, then picked them up. "The library's having a Christmas fair and selling off old books, so I thought of you."

A warm glow shone around Croaky. "Aw, how

kind."

Spike Feet held up her hand. "They're mostly kids' books, I'm afraid, but I know how you like reading the old classics so I thought you might like them. I batted them down to ten for a fiver."

They were chatting so much that I arched my back and yawned — one of those long loud yawns that really mean something. Croaky understood and let me into the garden. I was surprised to see Rat; he hadn't been around much lately.

His little pink nose twitched. "Haven't made a new tunnel, then?"

I pawed the ground. "How can I? The ground's rock solid."

"Down tools for winter, eh?"

"Well, I haven't seen you around much either."

"I live in a shed five doors down. Got a nice blanket on a deckchair." His black eyes twinkled. "There's a hole under the floorboards. The old man keeps seeds there like The Stick used to, and it's a ready supply." His whiskers twitched. "Why are you still here?"

I flicked a glance at the house. "She doesn't take me for walks because she hates the ice."

Rat stood on two legs and sniffed my jacket. "You're lapping up everything The Stick tells you. Never run, never fetch a ball…"

"She never throws one."

He narrowed his eyes. "Exactly."

"I bet you lie by the fire like a cat. Don't you want to escape?"

My fur bristled under the tartan coat. "Of course, when I get a chance."

"We make our own chances. You've got it too cushy; you're gone soft."

My back started to itch. "Everyone likes praise, don't they?"

Rat stared at me and his long tail swished.

"You've become an INSIDER. You have four legs and a tail, but you think you're HUMAN!"

"Of course I don't!" I stalked off and tapped the door twice so Croaky would let me in.

When Spike Feet had gone, Croaky patted me. "Did you hear that, Jasper? Celia's coming to my birthday party." She reached for her cookbook, but just then, the bell rang. She dashed to the front door. "Have you forgotten…?"

Slimebug stood there with a black briefcase. He looked smart in a checked suit and shiny shoes, yet an oily darkness oozed out of every pore. It made me wary, suspicious.

Croaky touched her chest. "Hello my 'andsome. How lovely of you to visit an old lady. It's my birthday on Saturday, so I'm baking."

He licked his lips with a slurpy slap. "A bit of cake would go down nicely. You have a lovely house, Maudie. What line of work was your husband in?"

"Arthur? He was a bank manager."

A sudden energy flowed into Slimebug; I could smell it. He reached into his briefcase and handed her a leaflet. "I've diversified into insurance, and I hear you've had an accident recently?"

Croaky wrinkled her nose, head on one side. "Wait a mo…d'you mean when I stumbled on that paving slab outside the surgery?"

His eyelids widened and he continued talking. "I'm sure I can get you a fat compensation payment. Can I know your bank details?" Croaky nodded, then she walked upstairs.

I stared at Slimebug. **What was he planning?**

His shoulders hunched and he tiptoed around touching things, looking more of a creepy crawly than ever. A growl rumbled in my throat, but it fizzled when Croaky came back.

"Sorry, can't find the dratted things."

Slimebug's smile didn't slip, but his nostrils flared, and I sensed a storm raging.

She chewed her lip. "I've just remembered what Arthur said if someone asks for money." She looked at her red slippers.

"Yes of course. You can't be too careful." He nodded. "So many sharks around these days."

When the door shut, Croaky twisted his little card in her hands. "What do you think, Jasper? I'd ask Celia, but the old trout always suspects the worst. No, we need to invest our money wisely so you can keep having your designer jackets, don't we?"

My ears pricked as something fell onto the mat. The envelope smelt sweet. I sniffed it all over and gave Croaky the envelope. Her head went from side to side, then she snorted. "I can't believe that wretched girl is *still* writing. Her parents have backed off, so why won't she?"

I nosed the letter, and she pushed my snout away.

Then she looked at the picture on the wall and sighed. "Oh, alright..."

> It was my birthday yesterday and I got some cool stuff, but all I really want is you, Bandit. I can't believe it's been six months since she refused to give you back.

Croaky sucked in through her teeth like the paper had stung her. She covered her mouth and I saw staring eyes. Now her chest was shaking. What was wrong? I started to whine. When she didn't react, I pawed her arm and the letter shook in her hand. She blinked several times and wiped her mouth. Then raised her shoulders and began to read again.

> Dad did this beautiful painting of you and I look at it every night. Oh, and I got picked for the athletics team — 800m — see, I still like running. Sometimes I think I see you on the beach and I sprint so fast, I'm flying. But it's never you.
>
> I'm sitting in our new conservatory overlooking the sea, you'd love it! Remember how you used to chew the

Croaky sank back into the chair. "Just like Joey —
his room was a pigsty." She kept blinking and sniffing,
and her eyes were leaking. "Perhaps I was wrong…"

All day she kept darting little glances at me. I was glad
when it was storytime; I needed her words to wash over
me. Croaky ran her finger along the new books. "We've
already read Heidi and The Secret Garden…" She
fumbled through the pile. "Let's try this one." She
gasped. "No, *not* Goodnight Mr Tom! I'm *not* reading
this one."

Her eyes were wide, with white all around them.
"He…he was like Tom's mother…whenever I did
something wrong, he shut me in my room." Her words
were quiet, but I sensed a great wave rearing up as she

took another breath. "He hit Mummy too. Sometimes I'd hear Mummy cry out. But no one helped. No one knew." Pain was swirling and crashing inside Croaky like waves smashing against rocks.

Her fingers tugged my fur. "He fixed black bars on my window, four of them, so I couldn't get out. I'd hear him stamping up the stairs..." She sucked in and her whole body shook. I'd never seen Croaky behaving so strangely.

Then she swayed onto her feet. "Oh, there you are, Jasper. Turn out the lights, dear."

I stood on a chair and batted the switch with my paw, then followed her upstairs. I nestled on my pillow and closed my eyes. I wanted to please Croaky so she didn't shut me in the cupboard.

Not that she ever did now, it was just a fear.

And fears can linger.

21. Another Heartbeat

The buzzing in the sky was back. The tall trees were empty now and Rat had disappeared to his shed. Everything shut down in the garden, but inside it was alive. Sparkling lights and paper rings were strung across the ceiling and Box Man had brought a little tree in a pot. The house smelt of lemony soap and my paws kept sliding on the floor. The table was laid with the best china cups and a massive Victoria sponge, oozing with jam and butter-cream.

Croaky leant on the table and cupped her chin in her hands. "We didn't celebrate last Christmas, but now that you're really mine, we can go to town." She smiled. "I remember the day you came to live with me. You looked so little and lost. And even though you're eighteen months older, you're just as cute with your long ears and your gorgeous ginger coat. It's been worth going to the Pamper Parlour every fortnight. We have to keep up appearances, especially as Celia's coming for tea."

TEA! My ears pricked up.

I looked at the cake, but Croaky kept looking at the clock. Then the phone beeped. Her chair scraped back as she leant across to the sideboard. When she looked at the phone, her cheeks fell into deep folds. "I know she hasn't seen her daughter for ages, but…" Her crackly breathing got faster. "Not even for my birthday." Her lips were wobbling, and I sensed a deep need. "*And* I made my own clotted cream."

I jumped down and leant against Croaky's legs, then she held out her arms and I climbed onto her lap. Her arms were trembling. "You'd always come and see me, wouldn't you Jasper? You're my best friend in the whole wide world." I snuggled closer and her eyes leaked onto my fur. I didn't know what was happening, but I knew that she needed me.

I only moved when she elbowed me as she pushed her glasses up her nose. "They wanted you back in July — or was it last August? But I love you, too, don't I?" She twirled my ear around her fingers. "I may have laid it on a bit thick, but they gave in at last. Besides, I heard that Isla's mother is teaching full-time now, and Joey's working in an art shop in Padstow. You couldn't be left on your own all day, could you?"

She let go of me to scratch her nose. "You get me through the dark days, you really do. I've not spoken to a single soul all week apart from you." Her jaw twitched and she reached for a knife. Then she sang in a wobbly voice.

"Happy Birthday to me,
Happy Birthday to me!
Happy Birthday Dear Maudie,
Happy Birthday to me!"

The light dazzled and the smell raced into my eyes. Croaky put her arms around my neck. "Let's make a wish. Your Mr Happy duvet is wearing a bit thin…or how about a collar studded with diamonds?" She closed her eyes, and her breathing grew heavy. "I've made mine."

The doorbell woke me.

"W…wasap?" said Croaky's blurry voice. "Oh yes, I ordered a takeaway." Her lips tightened. "As we waited so long for the old trout."

When she opened the trays, my nose started to drip. Now I love onion bhajis and I adore chicken korma, but any stronger and my mouth stings like fire and my stomach goes **Jiggly-Wiggly**. And as for my poo — don't go there!

The sauce was a bit **Sloppy-Slurpy** and the meat was a bit **Mushy-Slushy**, but it was tasty.

After we'd eaten, Croaky's fingers were stained yellow, so I carried the packaging to the recycling bucket by the door, and dropped it in. She smiled. "You're a marvel, Jasper, I think you could do anything." She stroked my head, my ears, then my belly.

Ooo, this is nice! I rolled over, legs in the air. The gurgling in my stomach disappeared as waves of pleasure surged through me. Croaky's face grew closer — upside down, but closer. Her spicy scent was strong as she breathed out. "I can feel your heart beating."

She looked deep into my eyes, but her eyelids kept blinking and her lips wobbled. "Don't you worry about silly old me. It just means so much — another heartbeat. The only other time I touch another living being is when the shop assistant gives me change."

We gazed at each other, then I heard the doorbell. Croaky held up her hand. "Snootface must've come to apologise." She hobbled over and opened the door.

The first thing I saw was sharp, shiny shoes, then long legs in checked, brown trousers. My hackles rose as Slimebug whipped a bottle from behind his back. Croaky clasped it against her chest. "Oh, but how did you…?"

He peered into the hall. "You said your friend was coming?"

Sparks of anger were flying off Croaky. And sadness.

"You c…an't celebrate on your own, c…an you?" Slimebug took funny little breaths then he sneezed.

Croaky gestured with the bottle. "I've swept the house from top to bottom, but perhaps Jasper has shed a little."

"A little!" said Slimebug, glaring at me. He puffed a little tube up his nostrils. "Just as well I brought my inhaler."

"Sorry about that. Won't you come in?" said Croaky, leading him towards the Fire Room. Slimebug slid along the wall, leaving a trail of gloopy sludge. You couldn't see it, but the smell was clogging my nostrils, making me scared. When Croaky sank into the sofa, Slimebug poured the drink into her glass. He kept refilling it and her eyelids began to flicker. Her chin rested on her chest, and she started to snore.

He tiptoed to the cabinet. "Now, where does Droopy Drawers keep it?"

The air was getting thicker, oppressive. My whiskers flattened and I felt anxious. Why was Slimebug nosing around?

Just as he pulled down the lid, I let off a fart. He lashed out and kicked me. I shrank back, whimpering in pain. Then I ran back to Croaky.

WUFF! WUFF! WAKE UP!

She swayed onto her feet. "Jasper, what is it?"

Slimebug glanced at Croaky. His eyelids narrowed, then he pursed his lips as he pointed at me. "Your dog made a horrible smell, and when I tried to waft the stink away, he bit me!" He pulled up his trouser leg. "See, here are the bite marks."

Croaky gasped. She grabbed my collar and dragged me along the corridor. The air was pulsing with danger.

This is all wrong. I'm trying to protect her, and she locks me in the cupboard.

Darkness dug into me, telling me I'd never be free. Then Croaky's slurpy footsteps grew louder again and the door opened. "He's gone… perhaps I overreacted… I'm so sorry Jasper…"

I lay with my head between my paws and refused to look at her. **You can hardly expect me to jump for joy when you just shouted at me.**

Croaky kept muttering. "I've been going over and over it. The bite mark on Mr Brown's leg didn't look fresh, it was dried up and brown." Her head started to shake. "I punished you for *nothing*. Just like that horrible mother in Goodnight Mr Tom."

I looked up with sad eyes. **I was only trying to help.**

Croaky's eyelids stretched so I could see the whites. "Why did I *ever* shut you in the cupboard? You were only a puppy — how could you know how to behave? You didn't do anything wrong. It was *my* fault, not yours."

She clasped her mouth and her stick clattered to the floor. *"No, I couldn't have…"*

She backed away and collapsed on the stairs. *"I behaved just like my father.* I shut you in the cupboard with no food. I love you so much and you mean everything to me. But I punished you for disobedience like he used to punish me."

She sounded so anxious that I crept out. Her elbow

dug into me as she lifted her face. "Oh Jasper, can you ever forgive me? I never meant to hurt you. I was only trying to help you learn." She stroked my fur. "How could I have done that to you? You're the best thing that's ever happened to me, the only one who really listens."

Her pain poured into me. Whispering things I couldn't understand.

After a long time, she clasped the bannister and stood up, then walked into the Fire Room. When I peered in, she was standing beside the cabinet. "I should have given this to you ages ago. I don't know why I didn't really." She held out a piece of cloth. "It's your cuddly blanket."

Familiar scents poured into me. Seaweed and sand and something sweet that dived inside me and jumped for joy. I nosed the material and couldn't stop wagging my tail. The salty seaside scents reminded me of splashing into the waves and dashing out again. Fun times playing on the sand. **My Forever Family. Home.**

Wrinkled hands touched my neck as Croaky tied the bandana. Other hands used to do this, soft young hands. An image flashed into my mind. **ISLA!**

We were on a beach and we ran like the

wind. How could I have forgotten my mission?

22. Sensing Danger

I wanted to leave the very next day, but Box Man brought some parcels and Croaky was in a strange mood: all **Hopperty-Happy** and **Bouncy-Bubbly**. She looked different, too. **Wibbly-Jiggly** flesh wobbled in waves above her knees when she walked. Instead of sandals, she was swaying on spikes and holding out her arms to balance.

She faced the mirror. And I saw another Croaky looking at me. "It might be a bit young for me, and the top is a teeny bit low, but I think the pink brings out the colour in my cheeks, don't you?" She pulled some pins out of her head and grey straggly hair dripped down her back.

The **Not-Quite-Croaky** turned around. "That nice Mr Brown is coming round again this morning. He's had some exciting news about Arthur's investments." Her eyes twinkled. "I never knew Arthur had invested in a gold mine, but he went travelling before I met him, so it must be true."

Just then, the doorbell rang. Croaky spun around, then walked downstairs, clutching the bannister. Snow whooshed into the hall when she opened the door.

"Bye, it's bitter out there," said Slimebug.

"Aye, Boss. Yer nose is red raw, worse than Rudolf," said Flatcap.

Slimebug shook his hat at Flatcap, wafting snowflakes in his face. Then he plonked it back on and opened his arms. "Maudie, you're proper glam today, like a movie star."

"What, me?" Croaky fanned herself with her hand. Was it to ward off the stinky cloud around Slimebug? She ushered them into the Fire Room, then disappeared into the kitchen. I don't blame her. I stayed on guard by the sofa as an oily odour enveloped the room.

Slimebug pointed at me and his left eyelid flickered. "My guard dog would've eaten you alive if the blasted mutt hadn't run off."

"Was that after 'ee bit you, Boss?"

"SHUT IT!"

Flatcap giggled. "But this dog is cute, like, ain't he?"

"Cute?" Slimebug's forehead wrinkled. Then his eyebrows disappeared under his hat. "He could go for a fortune." He rubbed his hands. "But right now, we've got bigger fish to fry."

FISH! My ears pricked up.

He laughed. "Yeah, the old bat is eating out of my hand. I've been casing this joint for months. My drone's got a range of five miles and transmits real time images, perfect for a spot of you-know-what."

Flatcap raised his hand. "Can I have a go, Boss?"

Slimebug snorted. "I haven't spent a fortune buying this baby for you to crash it."

"You mean it's *not* a knock-off?"

"Quiet Smithers, she might hear." Slimebug spat on the carpet. Croaky wouldn't like that. I didn't either, so I growled. He stuck his tongue out at me. But he wasn't panting like I do when I stick out my tongue and he certainly wasn't laughing. He poked Flatcap. "Get the document ready."

Something felt wrong. My hackles rose and I watched the men without blinking. If you focus hard enough, other people always back down. I paced forward, backing Slimebug towards the table and the jug of flowers.

His head jerked back, then he exploded in a massive sneeze. "You… you…" The jug tipped over, splashing water on him.

Flatcap's shoulders bobbed up and down. "Boss, it looks like you've..."

"Shut up Smithers!" Slimebug dabbed at the dark stain growing on his trousers.

He jumped back as Croaky tottered into the room with a tray. She gasped. "Oh dear, has Jasper given you an over-enthusiastic welcome and scat the water over you? He's usually so careful."

Slimebug smiled through clamped teeth, his free hand clenching in a fist. "Nothing to worry about. You're looking lovely today, Maudie."

Flatcap spluttered into his hand. How rude, couldn't he use a tissue? I lapped up the water soaking into the carpet and looked at Croaky for approval, but she'd turned all giggly. "I've not worn a mini skirt for donkey's years, so perhaps it's a bit..."

Flatcap gave a screechy giggle, and Slimebug glared at him. Then he clicked his fingers, so I sat. "No, not *you*, mutt!" He beckoned to Flatcap who uncurled a sheet of paper, then he pushed a pen into Croaky's hands. "Sign here and you'll get the money from your husband's shares in the diamond mine."

Croaky tapped the pen. "I thought you said it was a gold mine?"

Slimebug coughed. "Yes, that too." Excitement was chasing around his body. Fingers drumming on thighs. Little glances at Flatcap, behind Croaky's back. The energy passing between the two men didn't smell good. My hackles were stiff as a prickly hedge, and my tail was as firm as a stick.

And what do you do when you sense danger? I needed to warn Croaky, so I offered my paw. Her pen wobbled, and the paper wafted onto the floor.

"Get it!" said Slimebug.

I pounced.

"NO, NOT YOU!"

The shout scared me, so I clenched the paper tighter, and cowered under Croaky's skirt. Except I couldn't, as it was above her knees. She bent down and held out her hand. "It's alright, Jasper, please give it to him."

A pointed shoe hovered above my snout. "She said: Drop!"

DROP! Of course I understood Slimebug's command, but his tone was sharp, unkind. Croaky held my head either side, and looked into my eyes. "Jasper, please drop." My jaws slowly opened, and she caught the paper. "See, he was only trying to help."

The paper was whipped out of her hand. "Look, 'ee's bitten through the important bit," said Flatcap.

Croaky clutched my collar. "He's usually a little lamb, I don't know what…"

Slimebug growled. "There are laws about dangerous dogs."

I growled back and felt Croaky's body tensing. Then Slimebug backed down. "No bother. I'll print another document for you to sign."

She nodded. "Rightio. I'll whip up some cheese scones. Are you hungry?"

HUNGRY! I knew that word, so I sat smartly.

Slimebug swung around and hissed like a cat, then his eyes glinted. He spun back to face Croaky. "Better than that, Maudie, you've won a slap-up meal." He nodded. "You know the insurance policy your husband took out? Well, there's been a sweepstake and you've won a weekend at Jamaica Inn."

Croaky was buzzing with excitement, but I didn't trust Slimebug. His eyes narrowed as he nodded at Flatcap. "And we've got some business on Bodmin Moor, so if Maudie meets us at Jamaica Inn, we'll kill two birds with one stone."

"But Boss, you said no kil—"

Slimebug held up his hand, fingers splayed wide. His top teeth were huge as he pointed at me. "Smithers means no *dogs*." He placed his hand on Croaky's arm. "We'll have an early Christmas Dinner and tell ghost stories in the Smugglers' Bar."

"Cut-throats and dead bodies?" said Flatcap.

Slimebug elbowed Flatcap in the ribs. "Very funny, Smithers. He smiled at Croaky. "Jamaica Inn, Friday morning. Ten o'clock sharp. Don't be late." He glared at me. "And don't bring the dog."

When they'd gone, Croaky stroked my ears. "You're not just a dog, you're my best friend." She lifted her arms and they smelt musky like her dirty wash basket. "Just think of it, Jasper, we could do anything, go anywhere. I haven't had a holiday since…well, as long as I can remember." Her feet did a little dance, then she sang a tune as she climbed upstairs. *"Money, money, money, in a rich man's world..."*

I heard cupboard doors opening and closing, and a groan as Croaky wrestled with something heavy. Then a suitcase banged down each stair with a *bump, bump, bump*. The sound dug into my mind. Something bad was going to happen.

23. Showdown at Jamaica Inn

Croaky's trembling hands plugged in my seatbelt. She'd taken ages to get ready and kept coming out in different clothes, asking questions. She'd been so busy that she hadn't dressed me in anything except my bandana that I always wore now, but I wasn't complaining. I felt more like the old me. Perhaps something good was going to happen, after all.

I fought gurgling sickly feelings as the car lurched along, so I was glad when the window slid down. I pressed my nose through the gap, and a rush of wonderful scents flooded into me. The crisp cold air of winter sent messages in the wind. I tried to catch them, but they flew past. Then the world stopped whizzing by.

Croaky looked at me and her mouth squished to one side. "This is it: Jamaica Inn." She clamped one hand on her head to stop the hairball flying away. A plastic beaker skated along the ground, and she whacked it with her stick. Then she shivered. "I'm not surprised no one's sitting outside, it's brass monkeys out here." She tucked her handbag over her arm and clipped on my lead. "We'll get our cases later. That nice Mr Brown will be waiting for us. This is our lucky day."

We walked past other parked cars, then I smelt the foul odour of rotten eggs. A white van slid open and Slimebug slithered out. "Maudie, you came!" My fur rose to greet them, but not in a good way. I sensed something bad, a sticky smell of excitement. Flatcap stepped out of the side door and patted me, but Slimebug's lip curled in disgust. "I thought I said no dog."

Croaky fluttered her hand. "I couldn't leave Jasper. He'll be good as gold. Can we go inside, I don't like the look of those dark clouds?" She led me across the stone courtyard towards the building with sparkly lights above the windows.

Slimebug tapped a bench. "Two seconds. Best not let prying eyes see, eh? Just a couple of signatures and you'll be the proud owner of a gold mine." He rubbed his hands. "Then you can warm yourself by the roaring hot fire."

I waited until Croaky had sat down, then climbed

onto the bench next to her. I eyed the left-over chips, but I knew what would happen if I dared take one.

Slimebug and Flatcap sat opposite, and little glances passed between them. **What were they hiding?**

Our drinks arrived, but there was no cup for me. Croaky noticed and poured some of the bubbly stuff onto the tray. "Just this once Jasper, as it's a celebration." When she said this, I spotted Slimebug raising his eyebrows at Flatcap. I lapped the drink, and my nostrils went all fuzzy and a burp jumped out.

Slimebug glared at me, but it wasn't my fault, it was the drink. He spread some paper on the table, and slammed his hand down to keep it from flying away. "Sign where it says Maud Mandeville. Here, here and here."

I recognised Croaky's name. And something else. **DANGER.**

I was on high alert as a shadow crept over the drinks and a pen slid across the table.

Croaky looked up. "And I'll get the money today?"

Flatcap coughed under his hand. "We'll transfer it as soon as we get back." He licked his lips and spit sprayed on his chin. "Then you'll have your golden nest egg."

"*My golden nest egg*…Arthur, if only you were here." Croaky clicked the pen.

Slimebug glared at Flatcap, his body tight, muscles on edge. A growl rumbled in my throat. His mouth was smiling, but I knew he was fizzing and crackling inside, about to explode.

"What is it, Jasper?" Croaky sounded sharp.

Slimebug muttered under his breath and held her hand over the paper.

"Wot did you say, Boss?" said Flatcap.

He grunted. "I wish that mutt would take a walk."

WALK! My legs felt all springy and I leapt up.

"Get your blasted tail off the table!" Slimebug swiped at me. I dodged and a glass tipped over and smashed on the ground.

Croaky started dabbing her wet dress, but Slimebug scrambled past her and stood on the table to catch the paper wafting above us. Flatcap stood up to see. "It's not ruined again, is it, Boss? We only needed one more signature to clean her out."

"*Clean...me...out...?*" said Croaky, in a frightened voice. She clutched her chest and panted in short sharp bursts. Her hands suddenly flopped onto her knees and her shoulders slumped sideways. Before I could stop her falling, she crashed off the bench, collapsing in a heap.

I slid down beside her, but she kept staring, her eyes not seeing.

Slimebug's nostrils flared. "You idiot! The shock's killed the old bat."

Flatcap's teeth chattered. He kicked the broken glass away from Croaky's face, and leant the back of his hand against her throat. "Phew, she's still breathing. Let's get outta here."

Slimebug glanced at the building. "If anyone sees, we'll pretend she's our old aunty." He bared his teeth at me. "Grrrr! Back off, mutt."

Fear was flying all around. Croaky was lying on the ground, and she wasn't moving. I glanced at the building...at Croaky...at the road...

FREEDOM! My chance to escape at last.

24. Lured into a Trap

Help! I barked. **Croaky needs help!**

A hand clamped my muzzle, jamming my jaws shut. It hurt.

Flatcap's boots shuffled. "What'll we do, Boss? She hasn't signed the last bit."

Slimebug let go of me, and spun around. "Don't you think I know that? Who was the one who blabbed about cleaning her out?"

Flatcap swallowed. "Sorry Boss. It kinda slipped out."

"Well, I'll *kinda smash you in* if you don't follow orders."

Slimebug sounded snappy. Barky. I growled at him and stood guarding Croaky. Flatcap didn't like it either, and he gave a nervous glance over his shoulder. "Is anyone watching? If they heard, they'll be onto us any second."

I nosed Croaky's hand, trying to wake her, but her

fingers flopped back. I licked her face, but she didn't move. So I barked more loudly. **WAKE UP!**

"Smithers, shut that mutt up before he alerts the whole restaurant! We've gotta get outta here before she wakes up."

"*If* she wakes up." Flatcap's voice had gone screechy. "Then the dog will tell on us!"

"What planet are you on? Dogs don't tell on people."

Flatcap hovered in the van and pointed at me. "It'll still know."

Slimebug twisted his hands like he was squeezing a dishcloth. I sensed danger so I ducked under the table. His pointy shoes got within inches of me when I smelt the chip. His voice was light and sunny, yet I sensed darkness. But the chip was tingling my taste-buds and I started to drool. Then the chip landed on the ground. I crept out, but held up a paw, hesitating.

I don't eat off the floor.

Slimebug chuckled. "You want it, don't you?" A spidery arm reached forward, then he slammed his foot down and grabbed my front legs. And threw me at Flatcap. The doors banged shut.

A roar. The skid of gravel. What was happening? Ignoring the pain in my shoulders, I sniffed the edges of the vehicle. Flatcap shrank into the corner, and sank his teeth into a chip. I began to howl.

LET ME OUT!

Slimebug snorted and looked over his shoulder. "That damn animal is driving me nuts with that constant caterwauling!"

"It's not a cat, man."

Cat! That made me think of Polly and how funny it was when she leapt onto a chair whenever the cat word was said. But my friend wasn't here and it was up to me to escape. Thinking of Polly had given me an idea, so I leapt up with my paws on the headrest.

"GERROFF!"

The car screeched and we shot forwards, and Flatcap tumbled on top of me. For a moment, we stared at each other, then we got in a tangle of legs twisting to get away.

"What just happened?" shouted Slimebug.

"You braked," said Flatcap.

"That Mercedes got in the way. They've got a right dent now."

We shot off again, rattling and bumping. Flatcap was

panting and so was I. He squirmed and wriggled his bum. "Can you stop, I need the loo?"

"What d'yer think this is, a motorway cafe?" shouted Slimebug.

"I'm desperate, man, I'm gonna pee my pants."

Brakes squealed, and we were flung in a heap again. I thought Croaky was a bad driver but she had nothing on Slimebug.

The side door slid open. While the men were arguing, a thought flashed into my mind. **Do your famous run-though-the-legs trick!** Where did that come from? I was a split-second too late. Slimebug lunged, slamming me against the metal.

"Don't strangle the poor wee thing," cried Flatcap.

Spit oozed off Slimebug's lips, and his grip loosened. "*Poor wee thing!* You're gone soft, man."

This was my chance. I dug in my nails and slipped my collar, then did a flying roll and jumped out. The building had disappeared, and we were on a lonely road. I ducked down behind the van and heard Flatcap whimpering. "'ee might freeze out 'ere."

Slimebug snorted. "What are you, a weather forecaster?" The seat creaked as he climbed out.

"Where's the blasted mutt? He's our golden ticket."

His feet stamped closer, so I crept the other way. **Just like a game I used to play with the children.** But this wasn't fun, and my heart wasn't pounding with excitement, but terror.

"Here, pussy pussy…"

I crawled under the van, and lay still. Well, as still as I could with pointed shoes near my nose. The shoes walked a few steps, then stopped. Had he guessed? I did a quick belly crawl and hid by the back wheel.

His back creaked, then a hand reached under the van, clawing the ground. Before he could see me, I squeezed out and stood on the far side of the van, out of view.

The sharp shoes were moving again; Slimebug must have stood up.

"Did you see him, Boss?"

"As soon as the weather calms, I'll track him with my drone. He won't get far with my eye in the sky."

"Can I stay in the van? In case he comes back for some chips?"

I heard guzzling and lips smacking, but fear stopped me from investigating. Slimebug gave me chills, and he was so close.

"That's the first good idea you've had, Smithers. If we lose him, we'll stake out all the takeaways — and bam, we'll soon collar him again." Slimebug growled. "She'll pay top dollar to get her precious pooch back — she's trained it to do tricks."

"Yeah, like pawing the document so you didn't sign it."

The men started to argue, so I tiptoed around the van to the front. **WALK, DON'T RUN!** Croaky's command boomed in my mind. Heart pounding, I crept up the road.

I hadn't gone far before I heard hurried footsteps. I looked back. Slimebug was oozing anger. He picked up a fistful of gravel. "I'll get you, mutt, if it's the last thing I do!"

My fur was sky high. As he raised his hand, something snapped inside me.

RUN!

25. Alone on Bodmin Moor

The road turned into a rough track. Stones spiked my paws and the wind tugged my ears, but I kept going. Anywhere, so long as it was away from Slimebug and Flatcap. **What am I doing? I never run. Running isn't polite.**

I slowed to a trot, then held up a paw, uncertain, and was nearly swept off my feet. With my nose close to the ground, I ploughed on. Snow clung to my fur and I couldn't shake it off. I was exhausted. This was way further than walking to the post box and back.

But the post box was far away now. I sniffed the air. A bundle of snowflakes landed on my nose, so I did one of my famous shakes. If only Croaky hadn't left my winter coat in the boot. She might be home by now, waiting with sausages and bacon...pasties...scones with jam and cream…

I couldn't hear anything above the wind. It rushed at

me, moaning and whistling, then dived between some rocks. I'd reached a massive cliff which loomed into the mist. I climbed onto a ledge and found a little hole where I curled up. The wind was still screaming but it didn't drag me off the rock. I longed to snuggle in my bed; there wasn't even a cushion to rest my head. But when you're that tired, you can sleep anywhere.

When I woke, it was still daylight. A flurry of soft snowflakes drifted down, but the storm had gone. I needed a good stretch, but I couldn't arch my back because of the rock above me, and the giant slabs piling on top of each other.

What is this place, where am I? I clambered down onto a patch of soggy grass. Lifted my snout, and sniffed.

And a million scents flooded into me: decaying bracken and rusty heather, windswept fields and smoky houses, then further still, the faint salty taste of the ocean. A gust of wind rippled my matted fur, and excitement flooded to the tip of my tail.

I'm going to find Isla at last.

But all I could see was moorland. As I turned my head, a shaft of sunlight slanted towards me, warming my fur. For an instant, the tops of rocky outcrops glowed gold. Then the sun disappeared again. That meant that night was coming soon. And I didn't want to be out here alone in the dark.

I headed into a valley, and dipped my paw into icy water. *Whoooo!* The cold bit into me. I braced myself and pushed through, slipping and sliding on rocks until the ground rose under my feet. My teeth were chattering, and stringy moss stuck to my nose. I was desperate for warmth, but all I could see were stone walls and the odd tree bent over. I followed the scent of sheep, then saw them huddled together.

"Excuse me, I'm looking for a cottage with a door in two parts." The nearest sheep glanced at me and continued chewing. I crept closer. "May I cuddle in with you — just until I get dry?" The sheep kept chewing. **Fine, I'll take that as a yes.** But when I approached, she knelt forward on her knees and stood up. The others followed, tumbling over each other to get away. **Thanks very much, that makes me feel really welcome.**

I trudged beside the wall until I found a little hole. When you see something interesting, you have to explore — especially if you're in need of help. I squeezed through and fell into a wall of white. I kicked and pawed, but the snow was too heavy. Panic set in, making me pant in fear.

What if it caves in, like the tunnel? I'll be stuck here forever, and I'll never see Isla again.

I fought harder, my paws whirring so fast that clumps of snow tumbled down. I was winning — I could see daylight! It didn't take long until I'd burrowed through the snowdrift and dug myself out. Rat would be proud of me!

Mounds of snow were piled along this side of the wall. No sound except the wind — not even the bleat of a sheep. I'd never felt so lonely. I'd thought about escaping for so long, but now that I was actually here, it wasn't fun or exciting.

Maybe that's what happens when you escape? Or maybe escaping takes more work than you imagine?

I jumped back into the snowdrift and crawled through to the sheltered side. I'd freeze if I didn't keep moving, so I headed in the direction the sheep had taken.

After plodding for what seemed hours, I saw dark outlines highlighted against the evening sky. There was no nasty smell of Slimebug or Flatcap, so I crept closer. Rocks were sticking out of the ground like trees and more slabs were lying on the grass. A pony was rubbing her back against a massive rock. Her breath rasped and her nostrils were wide, her jaw tight.

I walked towards her. "What's wrong?"

Her eyes flickered. "What are you doing out here? Winter winds are harsh and cold."

"What about you?" I said. Her skin was stretched over her ribs, she looked ill.

The pony blinked. "I have weathered many storms. Go now, while you can."

"But I'm lost." **And I don't want to leave you.**

"Stick to the walls where there's shelter. I've had many foals, but you, little one, you weren't born into this." The pony raised her head. "Go now, before it's too late."

Hunger rumbled inside me. The strands of grass were bitter, but moistened by snow, so I chewed some, trying to quench my thirst. The pony whinnied. "Go! Another storm's brewing."

The clouds grumbled, then the sky roared and light flashed in my eyes. Shivering in fear, I crept next to the pony. She wasn't soft like a blanket, but she was here and I could feel her heart beating. I snuggled closer. I wasn't alone.

But I couldn't sleep. The wind was howling again, and something was out there. A large bird flew low overhead, the flap of wings alerting me. A scream echoed in the darkness, the sharp scratchy cry cutting into me. I curled up even tighter wishing I was home.

But would I ever see my home again?

26. Gunshots

When I woke, the pony's crackly breath was soothing; I wasn't alone. Birds were soaring overhead, their cries harsh in the wind. A crow landed on the wall with a loud caw. My hackles rose. I didn't like the way he was staring at me. Menacing. Was he waiting to tear into my flesh with that sharp beak?

He was trying to freak me out. I stared back, not letting him get the upper hand. **I'm a TUNNELLER, an ESCAPER, a SURVIVOR.**

Thinking of what I'd overcome gave me confidence. I jumped up and barked at the crow. "Get away!"

More birds flew down, their eyes glinting, then something rustled behind me. The pony rolled onto her back and kicked her legs. I thought that was my party trick. She stood and shook her mane. When she flicked her tail, the birds flew up in a squawk. She lifted her head and whinnied. The joyous high-pitched sound rang out across the moor. Her ears flattened, her nostrils flared, and her tongue touched her teeth as she whinnied again.

An answering call. The pony raised her head, her ears pricked. And a group of ponies came running towards us, their manes and tails flowing in the wind. When they reached her, she puffed through her nostrils like a cat purring. Another pony rested his neck on her, nuzzling her.

Time to go. I sniffed the air. A faint smell of salt. The sea! I scrambled over the rocks and scratchy moorland. Then, there were fields and stiles. I squeezed through a narrow gap in the first one, but the next stile had sharp, barbed wire.

Come on Bandit, you can do this!

I dug away some grass and tried to burrow under, but the wire scratched my shoulder and I smelt blood. I glared at the stile, then headed back along the fence.

Drizzle clung to my coat, then rain lashed into my face. My fur was dripping, and my ears and my tail dragged in the dirt. Puddles were everywhere. I sprang onto thick squelchy tufts. Then the ground disappeared. All I could see were spiky reeds and little bubbles.

ONE, TWO, THREE!

I leapt into the bog, my ears flapping. Now my

whole body was a muddy tangled mess.

I needed shelter. A path sloped down to some trees, then turned into a wider track. A house. No roof. Straggly plants climbed up the crumbling building. I climbed into the dead house, then gave a shake and the walls spun around me.

As I lay licking my wounds, the air grew warmer, and puffs of steam rose from the walls. I clambered out and rubbed my head on the grass, rolling over and kicking my legs like the pony. Then heard the gentle sigh of the earth relaxing. Tiny grasses stretching and earth loosening. Insects and bugs daring to move. Wisps of salty air wove into the smells of damp earth and woodland. Feeling more positive, I set off down the track through the trees. Today I would find Isla.

Before long, I heard rustling in the undergrowth. A glimpse of golden-brown feathers as a bird lifted a clawed foot. It was scratching and pecking tiny grains off the ground. As I crept closer, its neck bobbed up showing red patches around its eyes. I'd never been so close to a pheasant before. My legs trembled and, for a second, I felt like chasing it.

A loud shout. I froze. Footsteps crunched the

bracken. Sharp cracks like a stick whacking a tree. The male pheasant scuttled away, followed by some light brown females. The shouts grew louder, the noises more frightening. I darted after the fleeing birds. The trees were thinning. Patches of green grass. We flooded out onto a wide hillside. Crashing, clapping noises were right behind us. People burst through the trees flapping large flags.

The pleasants flew up, startled.

BANG! BANG! BANG!

The gunshots sent shivers through me. I wanted to escape, but the male pheasant was lying on its side, his glossy plumage slumped on the ground. I lift my paw, unsure of how to help.

Pounding paws. "Get off, that's mine!" The springer spaniel was the same size as me, but his tail had shot up, his hackles were raised and he was glaring with hard eyes. The brown specks in his white muzzle quivered as he opened his jaws.

I shrank closer to the bird. "Leave it alone."

The spaniel bared his teeth, hissing hot angry breath. I couldn't dodge in time and excruciating pain shot through me.

I growled and twisted my neck, trying to retaliate by sinking my teeth into his skin. Spit and froth. Jaws and claws. Then my attacker let go and snatched the pheasant in his mouth, long tail feathers pointing up and shimmering green and blue neck flopping. The spaniel ran off with his prize towards a line of figures at the far end of the field. Each one was leaning on their back leg, pointing a gun to the sky.

The flag men were shouting again, herding more pheasants into the open. I had to warn them before they got hurt like the male. It worked. Seeing me bombing towards them, the group split in all directions. The men yelled and flapped their flags, but a flurry of pheasants escaped into the trees.

A flag man stormed towards me, wafting air in my face. "That dog's not one of ours. It's wrecking the shoot!" The ground shuddered.

He swung back his boot, so I turned tail and ran. Away from the flag men and the wood. Straight towards the people with guns. As I veered to one side, the springer spaniel dropped the pheasant at the feet of a man with a club.

My paws tore the grassy soil. Beyond me was a

hedge, a hiding place. I tumbled through the prickles, falling onto softer earth. An odour hung around me, wild and musky. My eyes watered and I blinked. I lay trembling, my ear pulsing with pain. Then heard two heavy whacks.

Was that the poor pheasant? If I don't get out of here, I might be next.

27. Cornish Pasties and Sheep Poo

I sped down a track, weaving around bushes and dodging tree trunks. **Water...I can hear water!** I slithered down a bank. The water turned red, but it numbed the fiery stinging in my ear. I lapped thirstily. This was better than sucking moisture from the snowy grass on the moor. My body still throbbed with pain, but I felt clean. I cocked my leg against a tree. When you've nearly been mauled to death, doing a **Wild Wee** in a strange place doesn't really come top of the list of Bad Manners.

I kept walking. The landscape was flatter here, with more stone walls and a few stone huts. Sheep were clustered in neat fields, no longer scattered on the hillside. I was so hungry that I pawed a little round pellet. Croaky never let me eat sheep poo. But it smelt so good...perhaps one little pellet wouldn't hurt...

Mmm, this beats a **Nice Nibble** or a **Scrummy Snack**, it's a **Taste Bomb!**

I licked my lips, savouring every scrap of deliciousness. I was about to dive in for more, when my ears pricked.

A drone of an engine died in the distance. I stood still and arched my neck. In amongst the oil and car fumes, a delicious scent was drifting in the air. I increased my pace. Two people were leaning against a parked car near a bin with open sides. More food! The chips were already getting up my nostrils, they smelt

Tingle-Tongue-Tasty!

Croaky's voice boomed in my head, warning me. *We do not steal food! We do not gobble! We never drool and we never snatch!*

I approached the woman slowly and wagged the tip of my tail. She backed away, so I turned to the man and held out a paw. He smiled and threw me a chip. I stared into his eyes, willing him to swallow his first.

His eyebrows lifted. "Don't you want it?"

I kept staring until he ate, then mine was gone in a single bite. **More please?** He opened a packet of biscuits and two fell out. Maybe manners don't count outside? I risked it and bolted them down.

The man stepped closer. "Look Lyndsey, he hasn't

got a collar. He must be a stray like those wild donkeys."

"They're not donkeys, they're ponies." The woman jingled some keys. "We've had our coffee, let's go, it's freezing."

"But he's wearing a bandana, he must belong to someone. Dogs don't randomly dress themselves, do they?" The man knelt and held out his hand. "We can't just leave him, he'll freeze to death."

The woman honked the car horn. "Leave it alone, Darren. It'll be crawling with ticks!" A biscuit wrapper flew at the bin, but missed. He didn't even bother to pick it up.

I heard Croaky's voice again. *Everything has a place and everything in its place.*

But right now, that wrapper was calling. When the car zoomed off, I licked the metallic foil clean. Not exactly beef bourguignon, but anything tastes good when you're really hungry.

My tongue hung out. But stronger than thirst was my homing instinct. **It's this way.** I don't know how I knew, I just did. More cars passed, leaving choking fumes, so I cut across fields. Pain jolted with every step, but I didn't care. I was going home.

When I reached a wider road, I heard the whirry wasp-bird in the sky again. Houses. A buzz of people. Food. I stared wistfully at a pile of cakes behind a window. A woman approached the shop and I lifted my paw — **Just one cake?** Her nose wrinkled, and she shut the door.

Next, I tried a vegetable stall. That didn't work either. When I approached, a man shouted at me and a volley of Brussels sprouts bounced on the road. I darted between shoppers and pounced on a sprout before it rolled in the gutter. Then I smelt a familiar spicy scent. Box Man was walking across the road holding a bag.

The sprout flew out of my mouth. **Hi, it's me!**

"Look where you're going," he said, as I bombed towards him. He led me back to the pavement and bent down. "Well, hello there, Gorgeous. Hey, you're wearing a bandana just like the one that quirky old lady gave her dog, the one who always holds me up and talks."

I gazed at him, and wagged my tail. Box Man ruffled my ears, then his mouth fell open. "No way! Are you trying to tell me that you really *are* her dog? What's her name? Mrs Devil or something?" He rustled the paper bag, and I licked my lips. He chuckled. "Or have you just smelt my Cornish pasty?"

My tail whacked his leg. He understood, and tore off a chunk. "It's delicious. Want some?" He chewed a small bite, then tossed the rest to me.

Mmm, Gobble-icious!

His mouth smiled with lots of white teeth. I nosed his hand, saying hello. His eyes twinkled and he fingered my bandana. "Where's your collar, then? No, you can't be her dog. She's precious about her little pooch." He rubbed the crumbs off his hands, and stood up.

I followed him to his car, then a movement caught my eye. A shadowy figure, scuttling spider-like low to the ground. He slid along beside a wall so tightly that he almost stuck to it. Another man emerged from an alleyway, taking sideways glances. I whimpered, trying to warn Box Man.

It was too late. I heard a loud sneeze. And saw those sharp, pointed shiny shoes.

28. Slimebug Gets Even Slimier

Slimebug leant against the bonnet of Box Man's car. "We'll take it from here, thanks."

"Our pooch ran off," said Flatcap, who'd popped up on the other side. "'ee's called Jasper."

I leant against Box Man's trousers. **Don't leave me with them!** He held up his hands. "Sorry, is this your dog? I thought…"

"He gets like that, a bit skittish. Once he's back home, he's as good as gold." Slimebug tapped a plastic tray. "Catch a whiff of this, boy, it's way better than greasy chips."

"He's already had a pasty," said Box Man. "Sorry, I gave him half of mine."

"Wot type?" said Flatcap, licking his lips. "My favourite's venison, stilton and rosemary…"

"We're not on *MasterChef*, Smithers," snapped Slimebug.

"Sorry, Boss."

Box Man's hand tightened on my bandana and I shrank between his legs. Slimebug lowered the tray, and hot flavours hit my nostrils. "Fancy a vindaloo?"

"Chicken korma's more my cup of tea," said Box Man, keeping hold of me.

Slimebug shrugged his shoulders, then, with a sudden twist of his fingers, he tipped the tray upside down. "Din-Dins!"

DINNER! I broke away from Box Man, my taste buds screaming. **Woah, this is spicy!** My throat was burning, but hey, it was food. I was just about to lick the sauce when *oomph!* Pain shot through my eyes as Slimebug grabbed the scruff of my neck. My body was throbbing and my tummy was going crazy, but I had no strength left to struggle.

The men were arguing over my head.

"And I suppose he knows *you*? Planning to nick our dog, are you?" said Slimebug. I twisted, and saw him making jerking neck movements towards Flatcap. Who looked at him blankly.

"Wot?"

Slimebug's eyelids widened. "*You* know."

I squirmed free and darted back to Box Man, who scooped me into his arms. His heart was booming really fast.

"Give him back," said Slimebug, "He's ours."

"Yeah," said Flatcap. "We've been staking out the shops all morning — " He stumbled suddenly. "Wot d'yer do that for, Boss? I only meant that I'm stuffed, I've eaten three Cornish pasties."

Slimebug grabbed Flatcap's scarf and pulled it so their heads were close. "I'll stuff you in a minute!"

Box Man gasped. He opened his car door and lifted me onto the seat. "Jump in, Jasper. You're going home."

HOME! I know that word!

Slimebug was still yelling at us, but I was in a car, and we were speeding off. I panted in excitement as we left the town. **I'm going to see Isla at last!**

I stood on the seat and watched trees and lampposts race by. I was panting so much the window steamed up. Then it slid down and the world rushed into me, in the way I liked. But I began to tremble. **The air isn't salty — we're going the wrong way**! Dribble ran down my jaws, dripping onto the plastic, but I couldn't help it. Why weren't we going home? The car slowed down and I caught some familiar scents. The playpark...the village field... Why were we back here?

The car stopped. The gate shut behind us, and Box Man let me down. The footpath crunched as he walked to the door.

Rat was hiding behind the bin. He winked. "Another botched escape?"

I stamped on a shrivelled teabag. "It was complicated."

He sniffed at me. "Oy, where d'yer get that curry, I'm starving?"

My whiskers tingled. "You wouldn't want it, trust me."

Rat flicked his tail. "You can't get a decent meal these days. All she left was a few measly crumbs."

Don't talk about food, my tummy's gurgling like a river.

A curtainy thing twitched in the Glass Room, then the door opened and Spike Feet rushed outside. "Jasper, where on earth...I've been worried sick." She patted my head. "Maud will be so glad once she..."

I tilted my head, then turned all waggy and bouncy as Polly bounded towards me and licked my face. "Bandit, I thought you'd found your family, I haven't seen you for ages."

I arched my neck and we touched noses. "I tried to, I was nearly at the sea when…" I stared at her leg. The bandage had gone. And she'd run outside to greet me, she was alright again!

While we were catching up on our news, Box Man strode over to Spike Feet. "Phew, so the cocker spaniel *does* belong to her."

Spike Feet nodded. "Yes, this is Maud Mandeville's dog. Sorry, who are you?"

He clicked his fingers. "Of *course* — *that's* her name. I often deliver around here, and I found her dog wandering in Wadebridge. He seems to know me, but he's lost his collar." Box Man rubbed his chin. "He looks a bit rough…I wonder if those two guys…" He glanced over his shoulder at his car. "D'you know when Mrs Mandeville will be back?"

Spike Feet bit her lip. Was she hungry like Rat? An eggy smell was drifting towards us, but she showed that she didn't like it, by shaking her head. "They're saying it was a hit and run…the barmaid saw a van scarper and poor Maud was lying flat out in Jamaica Inn car park."

Was that a flicker in the bushes? The stink was getting stronger. Was Slimebug there, or was his horrible smell still clinging to me? Anxiety spun around and a bubble popped in my tummy.

Polly's nose twitched. "Wow, that's impressive!"

I raised an eyebrow. "Thanks, it's one of my better ones!" My tension fell away; the rotten eggy smell must be from the vindaloo, nothing more.

Spike Feet didn't seem to notice the stink, because she kept talking. "Maud left me a spare key when she went away… she's my best friend, you know. This will be just the tonic she needs to get on her feet again."

A shadow passed under the lamplight. My ears pricked, but it was probably just Rat taking a sneaky look.

The glass door was still open. My water bowl was there, and I needed a drink. The warmth of the house hit me and I suddenly realised how tired I was.

"Aw, he's curled up in bed, poor little fella," said Box Man.

"Yes, he's tuckered out," said Spike Feet. "I'll leave

the conservatory door ajar in case he needs a wee. I'm off to the hospital to tell Maud the good news." She turned to go, but Polly raced into the Glass Room and stood beside my basket. Guarding me.

Spike Feet clicked her fingers. "Come along Pol Dol. Let Jasper have a nice sleep. We'll see him again soon."

Polly nuzzled my ear. "She's doing that clicky thing. I've got to go."

I gave a loud yawn, then looked up with blurry eyes. "It was nice to see you Polly." She smiled, then the flick of her tail disappeared into the darkness. I wriggled to get more comfortable and tucked my snout into my fur.

Their footsteps grew quieter. A few moments later, another vehicle crawled up the street. Then stopped.

Good, I need some peace. Just until my tummy stops grizzling. Then I'll head home.

29. Rat to the Rescue

A tail whipped my muzzle. Ugh, Rat was in my face! "Get off! Let me sleep."

Rat's whiskers twitched. "Probably not the best call."

"But I'm shattered. Flatcap and Slimebug chased me and—"

"Yeah, yeah, spare me the sob story. Those geezers are outside. I'd scarper if I were you."

I leapt up, and saw lights bobbing in the dark. A stinky eggy smell poured into my nostrils. Then the front door rattled.

"Don't worry, I'll cover you," said Rat.

"AHH!" There was a crash, like something heavy had smashed into the fence.

"Where are you Smithers?"

Oh no, that's Slimebug's voice!

A dazzling light shone at the glass. I cowered in the basket, but it was too late, the door swung wide open.

Slimebug whacked the floor with a coil of rope. "I knew the old bat was dotty, but she's actually given it a duvet!" He paced closer. "Thought you'd escape with that Asian guy, did you?"

I slid under a wicker armchair. The rope swished, then the chair squished against my back. My heart pounded. He was trying to squash me!

More footsteps. Light flashing across the floor. "Shut the door, Smithers. You look like you've been through a hedge backwards."

"A giant rodent attacked me. The stupid fence was in the way and I've got splinters all over."

Slimebug laughed. "Serves you right — should've killed the filthy critter."

It was like being trapped in the tunnel, except it wasn't rock, but a chair scraping my back. I was forced to crawl out. Slimebug reached for me, then he arched his neck several times and held his nose.

"Wot's up, Boss?" Torchlight spun over Slimebug's face.

Slimebug leant back then exploded in a sneeze. A vase toppled over and smashed. "Where's my anti-hi...his…histamine?"

I crept past the flowers — treading carefully because of the broken china — then sensed Flatcap staring. He really should do something about his teeth: there were several black holes and one of his front teeth was shiny like Croaky's gold ring.

"*Smithers*! Stop shining the blasted torch at me."

"But Boss, the dog's doing these strange dance moves!" Flatcap pointed at me. "I'll film it, then we'll get millions of likes on social media."

"Social med…?" spluttered Slimebug. "D'yer wanna advertise to the whole world? The cops could trace us. You heard that old codger, she's in hospital."

"Wot if she snuffs it? I don't want to go to jail. It's alright for you, you know the ropes, but I…"

"They can't nick us if we play our cards right," said Slimebug. He wiped his nose on his sleeve, then pointed at me. "Stop staring. Sit down and let me think."

THE COMMAND! Instant obedience had been drummed into me for so long — or was the fear of the cupboard? Either way, I sat down.

"Thank you," said Slimebug. Then he tapped his head. "I'll be as crazy as Droopy Drawers in a moment, talking to animals."

Flatcap rubbed his hands together. "We could use him as a performing pet and get on *Britain's Got Talent*."

"You fool, of course we can't. I bet she watches all that trash."

"It's not trash. It's me favourite programme."

"SHUT IT, SMITHERS! D'yer want the old bat to grass on us?"

While they were talking I edged along the wall, hoping to evade capture, but Slimebug slashed the floor with his rope. "Here kitty, kitty!"

"Ee's not a cat. And you can't do 'im in, Boss, you said 'ee was worth a fortune."

Slimebug snorted. "He *is*, you twit. Now we know she's still alive, we'll send that ransom note. Get over here, we'll corner him."

I growled, but my tummy was gushing and splurging like a mad thing.

"POOHEE!" Flatcap squeaked. "That's even worse than yours, Boss."

"Who are you calling stinky, Stinker?" Slimebug held his nose and kicked open the door. I dodged him and jumped onto the paving slab.

"Get 'im!"

They chased me outside and just then, I did a big squirty one.

"UGHHHH!" yelled Slimebug.

Flatcap giggled. "It's what dogs do, innit?"

"Not on my jacket. It stinks!"

The torchlight shivered, and I saw Flatcap pointing. "Now 'ee's peed over your trousers." Just then, a big one bubbled up and splattered.

"POO-EEE PONG-DROPS!" shouted Flatcap. "I reckon 'ee's lost his powers. Ee's just a normal dog."

"What powers? What are you on about?"

"But you said 'ee was special, like?"

Slimebug stared at me. Then — it couldn't have been timed better — my tummy exploded again.

"*Awesome!*" said Flatcap. "Imagine that on *Britain's Got Talent!*"

Slimebug wiped his face. "Nah, the stupid mutt's gone feral."

"But the reward, boss…you said we'll be rolling in it." Flatcap started to giggle. You *are!*"

"What?"

Torchlight lit up Slimebug's foot. He hopped about, flailing his arms. "I'LL RING ITS BLOOMING NECK!"

The rope lashed, but I headed for the **Whizzy Water**, swerving at the last minute.

"Keep your blasted torch straight, Smithers, I can't see."

I knew exactly where I was leading them. *WHOOSH!* Slimebug was soaked and a stinky brown stream was oozing off him. **Wow, that was even better than I expected!**

Rat squealed. "Bandit, over here!"

SMASH! CRACK! Torchlight spun in crazy circles. Flashes of broken wood. The gatepost swinging on its hinges.

Rat ran low to the ground, then stood on his hind feet and bared his teeth. "Oy, mate, cop a load of this!"

"It's the Giant Rat!" screamed Flatcap. He skidded past and disappeared into the night.

"And now it's your turn, Mister." Rat puffed up to his full height and raised outstretched claws.

Slimebug pulled back a spidery leg ready to kick Rat. My whiskers flared and I barked an urgent warning. Slimebug wobbled and twisted around, trying to see me. A growl burnt the back of my throat, and it exploded into a pouncing snarl.

He stumbled and fell backwards.

Straight into the big prickly pot!

His legs were sticking up and he was clawing the air, screaming his head off. **What a result!**

Rat flicked his gaze towards me. "Don't just stand there — run for your life!"

30. Escape to the Sea

Streetlights are like massive torches. They lit up Flatcap who was jingling some keys and scrambling into the white van. The streetlamps also lit up Rat, who was running along the top of Croaky's fence. When he saw me, he stood on his hind legs. "I saw him off, didn't I? Should've kept their snouts out of our garden." His eyes glinted in the light. "The other geezer's stuck in the bush with thorns in his butt!"

I grinned. "We're a good team, thanks Rat."

I headed to the field where I paused by the bench, my nostrils twitching. **Yes, this is the way to the sea.** It was pitch-black in the wood so I trod carefully, following the sound of water. My tummy was still churning, and I needed a drink, but the river was rushing too fast. So, I curled up in the bushes, listening to noises of the night.

The song of a blackbird woke me. A pinecone was bobbing in the river and on the far side, the bird was perched in a tree. I slithered down the bank then launched out, claws wide, fighting the water. It stung, but it also soothed, and I was tempted to stay in. Then I remembered Slimebug's lashing whip. He might be tracking me.

I sprayed a perfect arc of water drops over the bank. The blackbird sang like he was impressed, but I left him and headed along the earthy path. It led out of the wood and along the edge of fields. Past an old farmhouse. Squawking chickens with fierce eyes, vicious beaks and scratchy claws. I nipped by, then followed my nose downhill onto a wide path. More trees.

People were walking towards me. One started to run. For an anxious moment I thought it was Slimebug, but it was another shouty man. He blocked me, legs apart. "Don't they know dogs must be on leads on the Camel Trail?"

I dived through his legs and did a cool roly poly. It's amazing how fast you can run when you're being pursued. Even when your hip is biting with pain. After I'd lost him, I gave up and hobbled. I sniffed the ferns and leaf mould for signs of friends. No one I knew. But I caught a waft of salty air, and a ripple of joy rushed through me.

A man whizzed past on a bicycle, his dog running alongside. The bicycle had a dog crate attached behind, so I forced my legs to work harder until I caught up.

"Can I have a lift?"

The dog didn't answer.

Fine, if that's the way you want to play it. I tried to keep pace, but the bicycle got smaller and smaller, and my legs got more and more tired.

They'd stopped. The dog was squatting on the edge of the path. **Come on, can't you be more discreet?** Then I realised this was my chance. I crept up to the cart. The dog was still doing his thing and the man was spitting at a plastic poo bag, trying to open it. Ignoring the pain in my hip, I jumped into the crate, and hid under the cover.

A crinkly crackle. The man's voice. "Stop messing around, Rufus, I can't stop every minute." The crate shook. "Keep running then, but you won't get a rest until we get to Wadebridge."

We were moving: bars on three sides, a canopy

hiding the sky. I sank onto my right side and faced the open door. Pain pulsed through my hip so I rolled onto the other side, but now my bitten ear was squashed. So, I lay flat out, head between my paws. Watching the track disappearing. And closed my eyes. For once someone else was doing the work, and I was tired of running.

Car fumes slid down my throat, waking me. The track had disappeared, and there were tall buildings. This wasn't the Pamper Parlour, it was busier and had a louder atmosphere. Then a familiar smell reached my nostrils. It was the Pasty Place — I'd just come from there. **I was going the wrong way again!** I stood up and arched my back, hitting the top of the crate. That was bad enough, but how could I jump out without rolling into the traffic? I shuffled to the edge and the dog eyeballed me.

"Oy! Get out. This is my ride." The dog yapped and snarled so much that the crate stopped. There was a shouting match between the man and dog. In the middle of it, I jumped. The snarly dog snorted and bared his teeth. "And don't follow us, loser!"

"I don't want to!" I spat back. But I was nervous.

Vehicles rushed by, and a motorbike stormed out of a passageway. If the dog didn't get me, Slimebug or Flatcap might spring out, too. I backtracked to a bridge. An inner sense told me that we'd just crossed that. Traffic flashed by both ways, but I was on the other side of the river now and it felt right. Perhaps the dog had done me a favour?

The rushing water made me thirsty, so I headed towards a row of bins, hoping for a drink. I found some soggy chips, but before I could eat them, my stomach did a squishy squelchy lurch.

"Ugh! That dog's pooing right outside the chippy."

Not more angry voices! I turned down a side road and cut across the town until the houses disappeared. Salty air was strong in my nostrils. And seaweedy smells. The sky grew lighter. I kept walking. Narrow roads with high hedges. Grassy fields. Then the horizon lifted and I could see the sea. And I had this strange feeling of leaping and jumping with Polly. I could hear her laughing and telling me to run.

So I did. And then at last, I saw a beach stretching out and touching the sky. I ran down a sandy bank and a million scents poured into me. My body was buzzing, right down to my tail.

I know this place! We came here in the car.

I raised my snout and more scents flooded into me of skittering crabs and birds skating across the sand.

I felt alive again. I'd missed this so much. I nosed the raised worm casts and lapped water, but it tasted salty. Funny how I'd forgotten that until now. But there were snatches of memories. Long walks along the headland. And racing the girl who ran like the wind.

Excitement made me jog faster, despite my limp. Stones and shells and sandcastles raced by, but all I could see in my mind was Isla. I scrambled up a rocky path, my fur brushed by the wind. I dipped and climbed and investigated little beaches, and each time, my pulse raced faster. My instincts were buzzing, I was getting close.

A fishy scent drew me down to a village with a stony harbour. Men sitting on upturned boats, chatting and mending their nets. When I smelt chips, my tail wouldn't stop wagging. **I've been here with Isla and Harry!** I forced my weary legs up narrow alleyways to the other side of the village where I stopped, panting.

This feels so real, I used to come here a lot.

Knowing I was almost home, gave me strength. The

mossy wall, the molehills, all the old scents were coming back. I sped on and the footpath dipped. And there it was in the distance: the white cottage. I only had to pass that bench, and then, hiding behind those trees, was the door that opened in two parts. Joy flooded me.

I've tracked my way back home!

I gazed for a moment, then noticed the man. He was facing away from me, and his back was bowed like he was tired, but I recognised the broad shoulders, the way his head was turned to one side. My pulse raced even faster if that were possible. **Dad!** He always used to sit there with his paintbrush and pad of paper, looking out to sea. His painty smell had been replaced with musty tobacco, but I was sure it was Dad. I bounded over and nosed my head through the crook of his arm.

His hand stroked my muzzle. "Hello there!"

I backed away in disappointment. It wasn't Dad's voice, it was slower and deeper. He was like Dad, but he had more wrinkles and less hair.

The old man leant forward and squinted, then the newspaper slipped out of his hands. "Dark golden…a cocker spaniel…you must be Bandit!"

My ears pricked at the sound of my name, so I

approached him again.

Newspaper Man scooped up the crackly paper. "Maud must've come to her senses and given you back. Isla must be over the moon."

I didn't know what he was saying but he'd mentioned Isla, so my tail whacked the bench in delight. He nodded. "You're Bandit, alright. Why did Maud behave like that, eh? She was so kind before, giving a home to Joe when his mother got cancer and I was up and down at the hospital." He sighed. "Then I had to go and have that stupid accident and Maud stepped in to help again."

I panted, my tongue dribbling in excitement. **ISLA, he said Isla again! Where is she?**

Newspaper Man stroked my head, then he smoothed the bandana behind my neck. "So, where's the family, eh? I've come all this way to wish them Happy Christmas."

I was eager to dash off and find Isla, so I glanced at the path, but Newspaper Man's grip tightened. "Joe's probably got wind of me coming over and that's why he's taken off. He's a right stubborn-un, just like his old man."

Now I began to whimper. **Let me go!**

Newspaper Man held onto the bench with his other hand and bent his knees. "Help me, will you — gammy leg." The bandana pulled at my neck as he stood up, then he led me towards the cottage, swinging the paper in front. However hard I twisted, I couldn't get away. And all the time he kept talking. As soon as Newspaper Man's grip loosened, I wriggled free.

Then there it was, my happy place. I ran to the door and jumped up with both paws like I used to.

Surprise! It's me, Bandit!

But the top half didn't fly open. No smiling faces. No laughing children. I dashed to the back door, and it smelt of fresh paint. Where were they?

I could smell Isla everywhere: her hands touching the handle, her hair brushing the window frame, her feet on the grass, her breath in the air. I nudged the door, then barged with my shoulder. When it didn't open, I barked.

Hurry up, let me in!

When no one came out, I barked even louder. Perhaps they were watching TV and hadn't heard me. Nothing happened. I grew anxious and scratched the door, trying to get in.

I've come all the way home.

Escaped from Slimebug and Flatcap.

Slept out in the wild.

Nearly been shot at.

Found my way back.

And no one's here!

An angry shout. "Oy! Don't scratch the paint." Newspaper Man ran towards me, waving the rolled up newspaper.

31.Tinkle-Tags and Jake

It was easy to outrun Newspaper Man. But I didn't want to leave. I waited until Newspaper Man wasn't looking, then I bombed back. I tapped the front door, willing the top half to open and Isla's head to appear. When the door didn't budge, I clawed even harder.

"Oy, get off! Stop wrecking the place!"

I jumped back. Anger was sparking off Newspaper Man and I didn't want to be hit. But my love for Isla was stronger. I crept forward, whining. Then I lay by the door, my head on my paws.

I'm not leaving. I'm waiting for Isla.

I strained for the sound of her voice or the crunch of car wheels on the pebbly drive. I'd bounce up and Isla would lift me into her arms and everything would be alright. We'd go to the beach again and run on the sand.

Suddenly I knew where she'd be. I leapt up before Newspaper Man could grab me. I headed back along the headland, on and on, up and down. All the paths and beaches I'd been to with my family.

Isla, where are you?

I was limping with exhaustion when I reached a long beach that stretched to the sky. No high cliffs, just sand and more sand. And lapping waves. A wonderful meaty scent drifted towards me, curling into the air. Two figures were sitting on a rug. I walked closer, wary of being chased again, but the boy held out his hand. His voice was deep like a man's, then it shot up again.

The woman tugged his arm. "Careful, Jake."

The man-boy called Jake wiped his mouth. "What do you think I'm doing?" His hand reached out again. "Here, do you like tomato sauce? Sorry, I've eaten all the burgers."

"That's true," said the woman. "You even ate mine."

"You were too slow off the mark!" Jake sounded fun, but his fingers were still hovering, and I felt a bit uneasy. **What's he want me to do, lick his hand? That's gross.**

Jake must have got my drift because he gave up and tickled me under my chin. "Look, he's got no collar, just this scarf thing."

The woman stepped closer and reached down.

"Well, he must belong to someone if they gave him a bandana." Her hand jingled as a bracelet slid down her wrist. It was a happy sound like my tag tinkling in my ears whenever I gave a good shake. I didn't know humans had tags, but this woman obviously didn't want to get lost, because there were lots of tags on her bracelet.

Jake stood up. He was tall. "We can't leave him out here all night, Mum, it's freezing."

"You don't have to tell *me* that!" Tinkle-Tags pulled her hat down over her ears. "Who was the one determined to have a BBQ on Christmas Eve?"

"Dad would have looked after him."

Tinkle-Tags fingered her bracelet and sighed. Then she cupped her hand over her eyebrows and looked into the distance. "His owner will be out there somewhere."

Jake gestured and his hair swept over one eye. "We've been here over an hour, and we've only seen one random guy."

She crossed her arms and shivered. "They've got more sense than to walk along Rock Beach in this weather — my ears are icicles."

I gave them my **I'm gorgeous, please help me** gaze — although my fur was tangled from sleeping rough and my wounds were stinging with salt. Polly would've said I needed a serious make-over.

The woman obviously thought so too, because she packed up the rug and walked away. Jake picked up a stone and hurled it into the sea. A dusty cloud circled back in a gust of wind. His shoulders slumped as he followed the woman. I trotted after them. Jake's voice kept dipping up and down like he wasn't sure where to put it. I did a **Please!** pose and raised a paw. I sensed I was winning when he punched the air.

Tinkle-Tags laughed. "Alright, we'll take him home tonight, but we can't keep him."

"But he hasn't got a collar, so he must be a stray."

"*A stray with a bandana?* No, we'll keep him over Christmas, but on Boxing Day we'll take him to the kennels." Tinkle-Tags swung the bag over her shoulder. "We'll have to hurry if we're going to catch the last ferry to Padstow."

Jake picked me up and I nestled into his jacket. I hadn't felt safe like this for a very long time. It was almost like being home.

I bounced up and down as he walked across the sand. We reached a wide river where seabirds with long curved beaks stood in the water. They flapped off when a boat chugged towards us, smelling of fire. I was glad of Jake's strong arms holding me, because I was exhausted, and my hip was aching.

Tinkle-Tags looked at me. "The poor dog's trembling."

Jake's arms tightened around me. "Don't worry, I won't drop you."

The boat was moving. Jake's hair hung over his face as he leant over the railings, and I nosed my head through the gap. Birds soared overhead, squawking for scraps. I arched my neck. **Home...it's back that way!** But we were heading across the water, away from the cottage.

I was carried onto a harbour smelling of fish. Tall gulls strutted around snatching scraps off the ground. I barked at one and it didn't even blink. I didn't fancy being pecked by a sharp beak, so I backed off; it must own this place. I was glad when we left the tall boat masts behind, and a car boot closed over my head.

I watched out of the back window, and the houses got smaller and smaller until they were far away. Trees and fields flashed by, then high buildings. We stopped and a door opened into a tiny hall.

Jake rubbed me with a towel. When my ear was tugged, I whined with pain. He understood and was more gentle. Then I heard several little high-pitched beeps and heard a word I knew.

DINNER! I wagged my tail. **Yes please!**

The meaty things smelt ok (Croaky would have given them three out of ten), but where was the sausage and bacon? I liked my new owners, but they gave me dinner in the hall. **I mean, who wants to eat off the floor?** I nosed the bowl along the floor, then tapped it twice to get their attention. They didn't understand, so I put my head down and pushed with my shoulder. The hard ridge between the doors was difficult to get over and one of the meaty things tipped out. I picked it up and dropped it back in the bowl. And heard Jake laughing.

"The dog's so clever." He knelt down. "Where d'you want me to put it?"

I stood beside the bowl and gazed at the table. Nothing happened, so I walked over to it, waiting for him to pull out my chair.

"What! Surely you don't mean…"

I wagged my tail and leapt onto the chair.

Tinkle-Tags put two mugs on the table. Then she

shrieked. Jake swept his hair away from his face. "I know, it's so cool!" He was on my wavelength, but Tinkle-Tags lifted me down. I stared at her without blinking.

"He wants to sit with us, Mum." Jake patted his thigh. "Here boy." I climbed back onto the chair and spotted a paper napkin, so I reached over and pulled it towards me.

I'm doing the right thing, aren't I, so why are you staring with your mouths wide open?

Tinkle-Tags raised her arm like it was stiff and pointed at the napkin then at me. "Do you think…"

Jake's hair nearly flopped into his drink as he nodded. "Yes, he's used to eating at the table!"

The bowl was placed in front of me. **At last!** My whiskers were twitching, but I kept eye contact with Tinkle-Tags. Her jaw dropped open even wider, but Jake just giggled. "I think he's waiting for us to eat!"

"But that's…" She lifted her spoon and swallowed, keeping eye-contact all the time. "I can't believe it: a dog with manners!"

Jake tipped some frothy drink into a saucer. Then he rested his elbows on the table. I tapped my paw twice to remind him it wasn't polite. His mop of hair started shaking all over. Then he pointed at me, his mouth wide open. *"No way! You actually think you're human!"*

I licked the froth around my lips and Jake laughed. "I'll post loads of photos and get hundreds of hits."

"You can't. Someone might see and think we've kidnapped him."

"Dog-napped!"

Tinkle-Tags cupped her chin in her hands and gazed at me. "Someone's spent a huge amount of time training him, and they'll be really upset he's lost."

After dinner, Jake took me into the garden to do my business. Then he threw a ball onto the grass. I watched it fall and flicked my gaze back at his face. He threw the ball again, but gave up when I showed no interest. He didn't give me any chores, so I stretched and yawned.

Where's my bedroom?

Jake didn't get the hint. I watched him whacking the ball at the fence, then we went inside. I wasn't given a bed, so I curled up in front of the fire and closed my eyes.

The next day we ate. I mean, all day! This massive dinner

stretched on and on. I had to educate them that dry biscuits weren't really my thing, but when I looked longingly at the roast chicken, I soon set them right. Jake sliced all the juicy meat off the bones and slid it onto my plate. I was stuffed! Then they pulled apart things that popped. Loudly. Jake put a rustly paper hat on my ears and laughed, his voice dipping up and down. I restrained the urge to paw it off, because they were wearing paper hats too, so it must be a custom in this house.

Then Jake offered me a parcel. He ripped the paper and threw a little ball into the air. "Fetch!"

Of course I didn't. Why would I?

When I stood there, he looked at me and passed the ball from hand to hand. "Do we have to take him to the kennels so soon?"

Sensing sadness in Jake, I offered my paw. **What's wrong? You were happy a moment ago.**

Tinkle-Tags brushed past me and put her arm around Jake. "Sorry, love, we must do the right thing."

Jake chucked the ball across the room and the door shuddered. I trembled. Something bad was about to happen.

32. The Raggedy Rottweiler

I was taken to a new place with a corridor of cages. A riot of smells and sounds. Barking. Growling. Whining. Howling. Frustration and Anger and Pain.

A small yappy terrier greeted me by standing on his hind legs, paws gripping his cage. "Hey, newbie. What's your name?"

"Yeah, who are you?" said another dog. So many questions. Different voices. Most of all, I smelt Fear.

Fear of being left.

Fear of being bitten.

Fear of being stuck in a cage forever.

Their voices jumbled, and I shrank closer to the young woman who was leading me along the wall of cages. We passed a raggy old rottweiler who glared, aggression steaming from his nostrils.

I brushed closer to the woman's legs, and she leant down to stroke me. "Aw, you poor wee thing." She scooped her hair back and tightened the two hair horns on her head. "I wish I didn't have to put you between Nero and Blaze, but we're full just now; it's always the same straight after Christmas."

The steel bolt of the next cage slid open. "Don't worry — Nero's more bark than bite, and Blaze is just a firecracker. They can't get at you; the bars are really strong." The door clanged shut.

I trembled and nosed the cold bars. **What is this place? You can't leave me here!**

"You'll get used to it." The voice on my right was high-pitched.

The cage on the other side rattled, and there was a horrible grinding of teeth. Was the rottweiler trying to chew his way out? I tried to block out the sounds and smells of **NEW** and **SCARY**. My new bedroom was very small — if you could call a rectangular cushion jammed at the back of the cage, a bed. No pictures. No sofa. Not even an armchair. There were two bowls on the floor. Where was the table and dining chairs? The view? All I could see were more cages in the opposite block: another long building with a scrappy patch of grass between us. Some dogs were lying in their beds, others pacing their cages like me. So many voices.

"Was that The Keeper? Where's our food?"

"Let me out! I hate being shut in here."

"I'm hungry. Why can't they hurry up?"

"Shut up, you always get yours before me."

The noise was constant. Sleep was impossible.

It was even more scary when Hair-Horns let us out into an indoor exercise area. Snarling snapping teeth were everywhere. Some dogs roamed the edges, but others barged into me, smelling my bum.

"Excuse me, please don't...I'd rather you kept your distance."

"Ooo, we've got a right snooty one 'ere! Live in a palace, did you?" The speaker was the raggedy Rottweiler, bits of black fur missing, all skin and bones. His ribs stuck out and one of his ears was torn. My own ear twinged, and for a moment I felt sorry for him. But there was no flicker of light in his eyes. Right then, I would've been grateful to be locked in the cage again. He was double my height and I didn't fancy being barrelled into by that massive chest. I trembled, but he advanced until his head was hanging over me. "I've got news for you, kiddo. You're just the same as us. *Unwanted.*"

The more he taunted, the more my tail tucked between my legs. **Leave me alone!**

A sheepdog bounced towards me and nipped my ear. "Don't just lie there or he'll have you."

I stared at the white stripe covering her muzzle. I didn't fancy being bitten by an overactive sheepdog. Or munched to bits by a Rottweiler. He stood, feet wide apart, teeth like cliff edges. I twisted to escape a hole being gouged in my neck, then backed against the wall, quivering. And gave a pathetic whimper.

Hair-Horns rushed over and raised her arm. "Nero! Blaze! Back off!"

The monster lay down instantly — **strange**. At that moment, he seemed weaker than me. Then, Blaze, the sheepdog, sprang at me, did a flying dodge, and whirled around, front paws down, ready to spring. Her piercing light blue eyes held me with a strange power.

"Can you jump? Are you a good runner?" When I didn't move, she raced around me in circles. "Bet you can't do that, can you?"

I didn't want to do *that*, whatever it was, her energy was making me dizzy. It didn't make sense. A lot of things didn't make sense. **Why were all these dogs together in one place? And why was I here?**

I was glad when Hair-Horns took me to get washed. The warm water was relaxing so I let her soap me. I wasn't too keen on the stuff she sprayed afterwards — it smelt bitter and plasticky — but I liked the long gentle brush strokes and her soft hands on my back. I closed my eyes. **Perhaps this place will be ok, after all.** She straightened my bandana under my neck, but when she touched my haunches, I squealed.

"Sorry, is it sore?" Cold liquid was spread on my wounds, then a pinprick pressed into my shoulder blades. The hair horns swung lower. "Just keep away from that Nero. He's only been here a few weeks, but he likes to throw his weight around." She scrunched her apron in her fist. "It makes me sick how some people treat their dogs."

I was back in the cage. Hair-Horns tipped some food into the bowl on the concrete floor. I say food, but they were just little round lumps. They might be munchy and crunchy, but there was no enticing smell, no taste.

I backed away and looked at her. **Where's my beef bourguignon? Pan fried salmon?** I would've liked to have trained her in etiquette, but there was no chair to climb onto and no table.

After I'd endured disgusting sounds of guzzling, the doors clanged one by one. Then mine opened. Hair-Horns smiled. "Exercise time for Blaze and her new friend."

This was better than the indoor arena where dogs stuck their snouts in your face and sniffed up your bum. You could get away from the dogs in the field. Except Blaze. She kept zipping down the hill, nosing around me.

"Bet you can't run as fast as me?" She raced up the slope then zoomed down again. "I'm a speed machine! Come on, race me."

"Leave me alone." She reminded me of Rat: pesky, in your face.

My cage was wet and stank of spray when I came back from exercising. "They hose it every day," said Blaze through the cage wall when the Keeper had shut us in.

"I'm not going to be here another day."

"That's what everyone says, but you'll soon find out."

"Find out what?" But for once, Blaze didn't answer.

Learning new rules was the easy part — I'm good at routines — but I didn't like the howling. Or the whining and scratching. Scared, unhappy, angry voices. It was worse at night, and the loudest howler was Nero. I lay by the door and looked into the darkness.

But it wasn't the howling or the whining that kept me awake. A strange bubble of excitement kept bobbing and ducking then rising to the surface again. It felt like an answer to a question I hadn't even asked. And it was bugging me. **What was it?**

33. I Am A Dog!

The next day, Blaze kept pestering me to play. "I can bomb down the hill and stop just before hitting the wall," she said, bowing on her front paws. "Bet you can't, can you?"

I didn't want to be rude and tell her what I was thinking, but these words were screaming in my head. **And I don't want to! When will you get the hint that I'm not interested?** I decided to investigate the fence bordering the field to find an escape route.

A crackle. Shivers raced up my spine. I spun around. And there, facing me, was Nero. My fur shot up. His head was bigger than my entire body and his teeth could have crunched me in one bite. Ok, slight exaggeration, but let's just say, he wasn't exactly pleased to see me.

"You're on my turf!" He sniffed my backside, and I cowered. When it came to that **treading on your personal space** thing, this guy was seriously over the mark. I hurtled back down the field, the monster at my heels. Fear makes you fast, and I beat him to the yard. But just when I thought I was safe, he made a massive leap and blocked me. "*What* were you saying?"

I crouched in submission. "Sorry, but I need to get away from Blaze. She's exhausting."

Nero's jaws frothed with spit. "No, *you* need to get away from *me*!" So I did. But he tracked me to the fence and patrolled up and down. "Don't you think I've already checked? It's rock solid," he snapped. "No holes, even for a pathetic scrap like you."

My legs were trembling, but I climbed the hill, anything to get away from him. The buzzing droning wasp-bird was back. I was about to look up when an arrow hurtled into me. *Oomph!*

"That's more like it!" yelled Blaze. "Let's do roly polys. It's crazy fun." I started slipping and rolling, but recovered my footing just before I hit the wall. "Not bad for a beginner," laughed Blaze. "Push *me* this time — if you can catch me!" She raced in circles making me dizzy.

And weirdly, something in me wanted to. So, I followed Blaze back up the hill. You could see the two huts and a road. The way out.

"Ready?" called Blaze. "One, two…"

My legs were tingling. As Blaze ran towards me I dodged, and she spun off down the hill.

Had I just done that?

She ran up the hill, panting. "Hey, that was a pretty cool move. Where did you learn it?"

"I…I don't know. I just…"

"You're way more fun than boring old Nero, you obviously like playing.

More fun. Like playing. Do I?

A growl rumbled at my back. "Shut it, Blaze, we don't all like fooling around."

Blaze winked at me. "Nero's a boring old fart, but you're up for a laugh." She pounced at me and stopped just short of nipping my ear lobes. "Aren't you?"

I pounced, imitating her. She barged into me, and we tumbled down the hill, landing in a tangle of paws. "We showed him, didn't we?" said Blaze.

Her eyebrows were so expressive and her personality so infectious that I couldn't help joining in. And I discovered something I'd forgotten. I wanted to Taste it. Touch it. I was digging in the sand and finding a whole new me. And it was racing around making me dizzy with excitement. **I am a dog!**

The thought whizzed and fizzed like lightning, showering sparks into every part of me.

I AM A DOG!

My heart pounded. I have four paws and a tail the same as other dogs, but Croaky conditioned me into behaving one way for so long that I'd forgotten. But faced with the explosion of scents and sounds in the kennels, **I was Awake! I had found My Tribe**.

I felt like a young pup again and wanted to discover everything. "How do you run so fast?" I asked Blaze. "Why do you race for the ball The Keeper throws, what's the point?"

"Because it's FUN!"

Suddenly the world was brighter, glowing with colour. Blaze was a great teacher. She zipped in and out of the exercise yard showing off her skills. I was a bit rusty at first as I had many months of training to undo.

Sometimes who you think you are isn't who you are. Sometimes you're pushed into things, and you become less than you are.

When you're taught to eat at a table and when you sleep in a bed with a *Mr. Happy* duvet, you can't help but believe you're a human. I'd been squashed into being a pampered pooch, then a lady's maid. But I was free at last.

It wasn't long until some cars arrived. The howling turned into excited yelps and happy whines. And waggy tails. "Pick me, pick me!" I ran to the cage door and saw people walking up the corridor.

A girl started to run. My tail started to wag. But there was no familiar sweet smell. It wasn't Isla. Then she pressed her hand against the bars. I tucked my tail between my legs, then trudged to my mat and lay down. The family walked past.

Perhaps I should have said hello? I knew I was a dog now and dogs have owners, but where was mine? Would anyone ever look after me again?

Then I heard more footsteps. A shadow slid along the wall. And an odour of rotten eggs drifted towards me. And I was afraid, very afraid.

34. Drain Stinkers

The slithery nasal tones ignited every hair on my body. But even more frightening than Slimebug, was the aggression steaming from Nero's cage, he was going wild, crashing against the bars.

"What have you got in there, a manic tiger?" Slimebug laughed at his own joke, and I couldn't help raising my eyes.

Flatcap elbowed Slimebug. "That one looks like your old guard dog, Boss."

Slimebug grabbed Flatcap's shoulders. "Keep your trap shut, *idiot*!"

"But it's you wot keeps dogs. I just have a—"

"Blasted budgie, yes I know." Slimebug lowered his voice. "But this other little guy is worth more than a million budgies, so play your cards right and you'll get a cut."

"D'yer really think 'ee's the same cocker?"

I retreated to my mat, my heart hammering. Why

were they here? What did they want?

Slimebug looked into my eyes and cracked his knuckles. "My drone tracked him here — look at the scrappy scarf."

"And the floppy ears..."

"I'll *floppy-ear* you in a minute." Slimebug beckoned to someone, and I heard soft footsteps, then Hair-Horns appeared.

"Found one you like?"

"Could I take a gander at this little cocker, Miss? He's just what I'm looking for." As Slimebug reached through the bars, a growl crawled up my throat.

Hair-Horns shook her head. "We're waiting for the owner to pick this one up. We need to give them a fair chance to respond, now that we've checked the microchip."

Slimebug rubbed his hands together. "Well let's hope you find your owner, poor little scruffian."

Hair-Horns' footsteps died away, then Slimebug jammed his finger through the bars. "I've got my eye on you, mutt — you'll not escape again once I get my hands on you." A bolt of fear shot through me when he shook the cage. "Thought you'd set that rat on us, did you? Well

I got rid of it pretty sharpish."

Flatcap giggled. "Oh yeah? I heard you screaming, Boss, and when I came back to fetch you, you had prickles in yer butt!"

"The stupid old bat shouldn't keep dangerous plants." Slimebug leered towards me. "But Droopy Drawers is going to pay big bucks to get her precious pooch back." He did a weird skippy hop as he passed Nero's cage. I heard a roar, then his footsteps bolting down the corridor.

My spy skills were alerted; **Nero seemed to know Slimebug**. I looked through the bars. "Did you see those men?"

"The suit and sharp shoes, or the flat cap and scuffed trainers?" said Blaze, from the cage behind me. "Why? Did you want them to choose you?"

My tummy went all **Squelchy-Squirmy**. "No way!"

Nero's lip curled. "Keep away from the Drain Stinkers. You don't want nowt to do with the likes of them."

My head was pounding, but I edged closer. "Why? What d'you know about Slimebug and Flatcap?"

His snarl made my hair stand on end. If it hadn't been for the bars, I'm sure he'd have bitten me to shreds. I pretended to be brave. "Who are the **Drain Stinkers**?"

Nero gave me an eyeful of his sharp fangs, then he rammed the cage. Perhaps that wasn't the wisest thing to say.

They came again the next day. Nero was standing at the top of the field and I was doing circuits with Blaze when I spotted them.

"Hey, look at Nero," said Blaze. He was bombing straight for Slimebug.

Slimebug screamed and clutched Flatcap. It took Hair-Horns and another Keeper to get him back in his cage — Nero that is, not Slimebug.

Although that would have been better. Imagine if Slimebug was stuck in a cage!

We were all punished by being locked away, which wasn't fair. I stood at the front of my cage and gave Hair-Horns my best puppy dog eyes. When she didn't open the door, I started to whine. That didn't work either.

Instead, Slimebug prowled along the corridor

towards Hair-Horns. He clasped his hands. 'Thanks for locking the brute away. Thought he was going to have me for dinner!"

Hair-Horns edged away from his sharp shoes. "Nero usually keeps himself to himself. You must have spooked him. The rottweiler's obviously had a rough time in the past."

Slimebug's nostrils twitched. "No worries, I'm looking for a little doggy, not a big brute like that."

"You spooked 'im real good," said Flatcap, who'd popped up behind him.

"I'll spook *you* if you don't shut up," said Slimebug.

Hair-Horns gave a funny high-pitched giggle like she didn't think it was funny. "Found a dog you like?"

The pointed shoes slid closer and Slimebug tapped on my cage. I hid in my bed. But when I turned around, he was still there. Pointing at me. "Could we take the cocker for a walk?"

She shook her head. "Not yet. He's been through the wars, poor thing."

"I can see that," said Slimebug, hunching his shoulders. "Some folk are downright cruel if you ask me."

I was relieved when Hair-Horns herded them along the line of cages, but my hackles rose when Slimebug gave a backwards glance; he was planning something.

As soon as Hair-Horns walked across to the opposite huts, Slimebug slunk back, low to the ground. "Get over 'ere, Smithers. We can still get some money out of the old bat if we play our cards right."

Flatcap joined him outside my cage. "I'm glad she's gonna be ok, like."

"Don't be soft. As soon as we break this damn mutt out we'll send our ransom demand, and she'd better cough up, or he'll get the chop."

When they left, Nero patrolled up and down the cage. **Fierce. Invincible.**

But his secret intrigued me, and I was desperate to know what he knew about Slimebug. I stood next to the bars that separated us. His **grizzly growls** got right inside me. I restrained my urge to bolt (not that there was anywhere to hide) and I said hello. His eyes widened and froth bubbled on his lips.

Blaze hissed at me from the other side. "Leave Nero alone, or he'll bite you when we're let out."

But I had to uncover the truth — especially when it

might help me escape. "Nero, do you come from moorland or coastland?" No answer. So I asked if he'd been to a village with a field and swings.

The cage shook as Nero butted it. "You get rescued, and you think you'll have a bit of peace at last, then you're driven mad by the scrap next door."

"Sorry, I just wanted to know…"

"What?" Nero's snout poked through the cage. Inches away.

My throat went dry. "It's about the…err…**Drain Dredgers**."

He gave a vicious snarl. *"Stinkers!"*

Yes, you do, I wanted to say, but stopped just in time and asked why he called them **Drain Stinkers**.

For a long time Nero didn't answer, then he sniffed. "Drain Stinkers hang around doorways, and they hit hard."

My legs trembled. "What happened?"

"None of your business."

"It's just that I know those men too. They're dangerous."

"Who cares?" Nero farted, and I smelt more than stink; I smelt fear. I edged closer and offered a paw through the bars. It was crazy I know, but old habits die hard.

"I do. My name is Bandit. And sometimes Jasper, but—"

"Stop gabbling!"

I took a deep breath. "Sorry. It's just that my last owner was hurt by the **Drain Stinkers**. She was sometimes cruel too, but she didn't deserve to be hurt." There, I'd said it. Nero stopped growling. And he wasn't headbutting the door either. He was silent.

"Excuse me...are you alright?"

Then, a deep, slow voice said, "Hurting is what he did best. He kept me chained up. I was always hungry."

"How did you escape?"

He didn't answer.

35. Nero's Story

I wanted to keep ferreting for clues, but I smelt burgers and tomato sauce. There was only one person I knew who smelt like that. As the smell grew stronger, my tail started to wag. The footsteps got faster, then a face peered into my cage. I was right, it *was* Jake!

He swept back his hair, and grinned. "I was right, it *is* him! Look, the spaniel's wagging his tail. He knows me."

Hair-Horns appeared with Tinkle-Tags. "If your son likes keeping fit, how about Blaze, here? A sheepdog needs plenty of exercise."

Jake glanced at Blaze then back at me. I gazed at the man-boy and my tail whacked his jeans. **You came back!** When the bolt slid open, Jake tickled me under my chin. He wanted to take me for a walk around the field, but after three laps, I pulled him towards the entrance. **Can we go now?** But Hair-Horns beckoned for the lead, then she took me back to my cage. I trooped in, ears dragging the ground.

When PICK-ME time was over and we were let out, Blaze spun around me, making me dizzy. "Why didn't you say yes to any of those people? You should have wagged your tail and given them the right signs."

I lifted sad eyes. "I tried, but the one I wanted went away."

"They always go away." That was Nero. He stood rigid and stared into the distance. I recognised that **Locked-in-the-Cupboard** look; I'd often felt that way. But I also knew that when someone is lost in their thoughts you can discover things they don't want to say.

Blaze cast him a quick glance, then fixed her ice-blue eyes on me. "Nero doesn't want to be chosen; he never tries to impress people."

Nero shook his ears. "No one wants a flea-bitten old dog who used to belong to a Drain Stinker."

"But surely, if you were chosen by a good owner this time?" I said.

Nero's back creaked as he lay down. "I don't mind. Here I get food and water, and The Keepers are kind."

I snuggled closer and rested my head on my paws. Nero didn't move away.

The Keeper walked by with Hair-Horns. "Nero is responding really well to your positive training. He's not spooked when he's with the cocker spaniel."

Hair-Horns nodded. "There seems to be a real bond." She leant towards Nero. "Have you found a friend at last?"

The Keeper smiled. "They say opposites attract. Poor Nero though. If we don't hear back from the database soon, we'll have people queuing up to take this little cutie and he'll be alone again."

🦴

That night, Nero kept me awake with a harsh cough. I didn't fancy playing when we were let out, but Blaze was having none of it. She ran around in circles. "Look at me! Whizzing is fun!" She was making me dizzy. When I heard her speeding towards me again, I rolled out of the way. She grinned. "That's better. Come on!"

I lifted tired eyes. "Then will you stop pestering me?"

Blaze wagged her tail, so I spun around, then went slower and slower until I sank next to the old rottweiler.

"That's shown her," said Nero, winking. I couldn't

believe it. I'd never heard him joking before. But he snarled when Blaze zoomed up, so she ducked into a ball and did a roly poly down the hill.

Wow, Nero had become my Minder! In a way, he reminded me of Polly, just scruffier, rougher and way more dangerous. I wouldn't want to get on the wrong side of him like those dogs who baited him and sniffed his butt.

But there was something pulling us together, the fierce old dog and me. And, looking into the distance, he began to tell his story. "He tied me up all day. Every day. When I growled and snarled, he laughed. I think he liked me growling and snarling at people." A sigh shook his body. "Sometimes I see this human in my dreams. They were kind, maybe even loved me. But when you've lost love, you can never find it again."

"No, you're wrong!" I said.

Nero raised his shoulders, and I suddenly remembered how large he was and how powerful. I'd just contradicted a fighter who could kill me with a single bite. But he just looked at me with blank eyes, like he had when I first arrived.

I stood up and sniffed the wind. "I know Isla's

waiting for me. Will you help me break out so I can find her?"

Nero shifted and lay with his back to me. He might have become my protector, but he was scared of letting his guard down. Without his help, how would I ever find Isla again?

36. Pick-Me Time

So many PICK-ME days had come and gone, when I heard a volley of vicious snarling. Slimebug was here again, and Nero was running straight for him.

"RIP HIS EARS OFF!" I yelled.

I was proud of my newly rediscovered bark, but it alerted Hair-Horns. She raised her hand, and Nero cowered a single bound's width from devouring Slimebug. The Keeper muzzled him. "Back to your cage Nero, there's a good boy."

Hair-Horns turned to Slimebug. "Sorry about that. I've never known such a strong reaction. He really doesn't like you, does he?"

Slimebug's lower lip curled. "Savage dogs like him should be put down."

I glanced at Hair-Horns, willing her to see how evil he was. Her forehead creased into lines. "Nero didn't have any other details on his tag, just his name. Are you *sure* you haven't seen that rottweiler before?"

"Course not, madam." Slimebug brushed a hair off his jacket. "I want that cute cocker, not a rotty who used to be a guard dog."

Hair-Horns sucked through her teeth, and her chin jutted forward. "Who told you *that*?" Her voice wasn't usually sharp. Had she guessed something was wrong?

Oh come on, it's so obvious! Why can't humans sense things like we can?

Slimebug's nose twitched, and he swotted it. "Everyone knows rotties are guard dogs. So, can I get the cocker?"

Hair-Horns folded her arms. "I think we've established he's not the right fit for you."

Slimebug winked. "Oh, I think I could wear him down!"

Hair-Horns gasped and there was a smell of fear. Her eyelids widened and her forehead wrinkled up like she was thinking.

AN AWAKENING.

She backed away and I heard her footsteps slapping the corridor. I wished Slimebug would go too, but he snaked out a hand and touched my new collar. When I edged back, he shook the bars. "You'll soon find out who the master is, just like that horrible Nero." He jumped clear of Nero's cage, then slimed away, creeping along the wall.

I arched my neck to make sure he'd gone, then Hair-Horns reappeared, panting. "Don't worry, that man won't be bothering you again. I've got a hunch, so I've just rung the police."

PICK-ME time was nearly over, and no one had come for me. Then, I heard a familiar voice. I ran to the cage door. Jake was striding up the corridor.

Have I been chosen at last?

Hair-Horns handed Jake my lead, and led me to The Keeper's desk where Tinkle-Tags was waiting. "We've had no luck with finding the owner. I discovered the flat is a rental property and it's changed hands several times over the last two years. I'm afraid the trail has gone cold." She looked at Tinkle-Tags. "We've reviewed your application, and you seem to be a good match, so we've agreed you can take George — we're calling him George for now— for a taster. If that works out, then this little dog could be looking at his Forever Home."

Tinkle-Tags clasped her hands. "That would be a blessing. Jake has really taken to the lovely little spaniel."

She gazed at the bracelet until the tags stopped tinkling. Her forehead creased and the corners of her mouth turned down. The next second, her mood lifted and she nodded at Hair-Horns. "It would be good for him to get out more, now it's just the two of us."

Jake pulled my lead. "Mum, I *can* speak for myself!"

We were nearly at the car when Blaze powered to the edge of the enclosure. "Bandit, you've been picked! I want to be picked. Pick me, pick me," she said, dancing around in circles. The lead loosened as Jake leant over the fence. He called Blaze over and stroked her.

Keys rattled. Key rattling is a sign that humans are about to go. But Blaze kept trying to win Jake over, poking her nose through the fence and licking his hand. "Take me too, you know you want to!"

I glanced around for Nero. I hadn't even said goodbye.

I know it sounds uncaring, but once I got to Jake's house I forgot about my friends. I couldn't wait to show Jake everything I'd learned at the dog place. All my new tricks. And most of all: **WHO I REALLY AM.**

Everything was new and exciting like I was discovering things for the first time. Which in a funny kind of way, I was. I bounded to the TV and stared, nose to nose with a dog on the screen. Then I bounced back to Jake, and flicked my gaze at the TV.

Look, that's like me!

He slid off the sofa. "I've never heard you bark before. You're like a different dog." He stroked my ears with gentle swishing movements, then touched my new stiff collar. "I don't know why they've called you George. I think you look more like a Archie, or a Charlie." I sensed Jake's emotions changing into a worry cloud as he looked at Tinkle-Tags. "D'you think they'll find his owner?"

She shrugged. "I don't know how these things work. But he's causing chaos in the lounge. Take him outside."

I raced in circles and tried to catch my tail, imitating Blaze. I jumped to catch the ball, but that wasn't so successful. When I finally caught it, I raced back and dropped it at Jake's feet and barked. **Did you see that!**

I wagged my tail as if I was happy. Which I was.

"Hey, you're a team player now," said Jake. He

threw the ball again, and I caught it in my mouth.

Dinner smelt wonderful. Jake patted the chair next to him, but I hesitated. This wasn't what happened at the kennels. I flicked my gaze to the floor.

"That's more like it," said Tinkle-Tags, chuckling.

I finished my dinner in seconds, then looked up.

Thanks! Any more?

She laughed. "Being at the kennels for a few weeks has certainly taught you a thing or two!"

"Let's go to the beach, see how fast he can run," said Jake.

Tinkle-Tags held up her hand. "Alright, if you promise to load the dishwasher when we get back. I saw a nice cafe the other day when we explored that cove up the coast. I'll have a coffee while you take George on the beach, but keep him on the lead; remember what they told us."

Jake scraped his chair back. "I don't need you to remind me about *everything*!"

We were in the car again. When we stopped, Tinkle-Tags went into a building and we went for a walk. For the first few steps, my training made me heel, then a boost of excitement whooshed into me, and I pulled to a thick clump of grass and left my scent as a message.

It's me, Bandit? Do you remember me?

Everything was coming back in wonderful whooshes of excitement.

Then something far more important happened, something that turned my life upside down and inside out again.

37. Alive with Sparkles

Salty air wafted my whiskers and I wanted to run, but Jake yanked the lead. Every few steps, he pulled me back, but my heart was racing. The rocky steps, the curve of the beach, the smell of the ocean...**I know the way, I've been here before!**

As soon as sand was between my paws, I arched my neck and pulled Jake along. My legs were tingling and my whole body was alive with sparkles. Running on the beach felt so natural, such fun. It was almost as good as being with Isla. When I was with her, we'd run until we couldn't run, it was the best time. And on days when the sea was hungry, we'd sit on the rocks and watch the waves.

My claws tore holes in the sand as Jake reeled in the lead. He sat with his legs circling me. "You love the sea, don't you, George? I'm so glad Mum and I moved to Cornwall when Dad..." His arms tightened, but energy was powering inside me and I couldn't sit still.

Everything felt so familiar. The squawking gulls, the sweep of the headland and the sea. I jumped up, splashing sand in Jake's lap. He crawled towards me and I gazed into his eyes, pleading.

He smiled and unclipped the lead. "Alright, but don't tell Mum."

I was free! I darted across the pebbles following bumpy worm casts, and I checked out scents hidden in strings of seaweed. I chased little crabs scuttling over the beach. I followed trails in the sand and left my own scent. I heard Jake shouting, but something had taken hold of me and I wanted to run forever. Birds scattered as I approached, flying low over the sand.

Then I saw a girl sitting on a rock. She was staring out at the sea.

I skidded to a halt. My fur rose. There was something about her sweet smell. The way she sat hugging her knees. The way her hair was dancing in the breeze.

She must have sensed me standing there, because she turned. Then my tail started to wag and it wouldn't stop.

It was Isla, my Isla!

She smiled. "Hello, Beautiful. I had a cocker spaniel like you, and he wore a spotty red bandana just like that one."

It's me! Bandit! Look, it's me!

I leant against her legs and nosed under her arm until she had to cuddle me. She stroked my head and my ears, smoothing them over and over. "You're so like him."

I wriggled closer and looked into her eyes. She gazed back, then covered her mouth with her hand. *"No, it can't be…"* Her eyes were shiny now. *"Bandit?"* She said the word slowly like it was made of something that could fall apart. "Bandit...is it you?"

And I knew I *was*. I laid my head on her lap and her hair covered me like a duvet. I snuggled closer to her warmth, finally home.

A shout. I looked up. Isla did, too.

Jake dashed towards us, then held his hips and panted. "Sorry, is my dog bothering you?" He crouched, wanting to pick me up. "We've just got George from the kennels."

"*George?* Oh, of course. Sorry." Isla's arms dropped but I didn't move.

"He really likes you," said Jake. He sat on another rock, and I watched his expression as he focused on Isla again. I may have wriggled closer, or she may have shifted position, but we were touching again, her hand on my bandana.

She nodded. "For a moment I thought...but he can't be my dog because *she* wouldn't let him go." Isla fingered my stiff new collar, and the tag tinkled.

My tail swished grains of sand. **I love you. You're my best friend.**

I watched every flicker of Isla's eyes as she talked to Jake, every lift or squeeze of her eyebrows. "How old is he?"

"They think he's two or three."

"Bandit would've been two and a half. I miss him so much."

"He died?"

Isla picked up a pebble and rolled it in her fingers. "This horrid old woman refused to give him back when we got back to the UK. Dad should have called the police. Then she sent him a text and he went all tight-lipped and refused to fight for Bandit anymore. It's not fair. We'd only gone for a year…" Isla sniffed. "I had him from a puppy."

Jake's hair dripped over one eye. "That's so tough. George is on a home visit, but I hope we can keep him."

Isla edged closer and stroked me under my chin. **Mmm, that feels so good!** My tail was happy too, it was making the sand jump and dance. I felt like bouncing around, but I didn't want Isla to let go for a second. Her breath shuddered.

"This was his favourite beach. We'd run for hours. It was the best time…" Her voice trailed off as she walked away. My legs spun, trying to follow, but Jake held my collar.

I gave a whimpery bark. **Isla, it's me, Bandit!**

She turned and dug her toe in the sand. "Dad lost his job, and we had to leave Exeter and all our friends, but Bandit was always there for me."

He nodded. "I know what you mean. My dad died a year ago, and finding George was…well, I think he found us really." Now it was Jake's turn to jump up. "Sorry, that sounds..."

"No, I get it," said Isla, walking closer. She crouched down to stroke my back. Waves of delight ran through me, and I wanted to stay like this forever, with her soft hands brushing my chest. I nestled even closer.

I'm here and I'm never going away ever again.

Her shoulders lifted, then her breath swished around me. Why was Isla sighing? She shouldn't be sad, not now that we've found each other? She looked at Jake. "Bandit was special, too. I think he understood everything I said. If only Dad hadn't been offered that job in Dubai, none of this would've happened."

"Sorry." Jake stroked my ear, then their hands touched, and they sprang apart. "Sorry," he said again.

"It's ok," said Isla. She smiled. And Jake smiled. I

didn't know what was going on, but I knew both of them and they seemed to be friends.

Jake swept back his hair as he attached my lead. "I'm Jake, by the way."

"Isla." Her name dived inside me and jumped around. **Isla, my forever friend!**

But why was she leaving? She was running, her hair flying in the wind. I howled and tugged the lead, but Jake wouldn't let me go.

38. This is me, Bandit!

We'd reached the edge of the beach when the scent of paint drifted towards me. Hurried footsteps. Isla and a tall man were running towards us.

My tail lashed from side to side. **Dad!**

Isla reached me first. "This is the dog I was telling you about."

Dad nodded. "He's a cocker spaniel right enough, but it's a bit far-fetched to think…"

Isla twisted her scarf in her hands then it fluttered onto the sand. Without thinking, I picked it up and nosed it into her hands. Like I used to. She stared at me for the longest time, then pulled it smooth and shook out a fountain of sand.

I ducked my head under the scarf. **Come on, see who I really am. This is me, Bandit!**

She pulled away from me, half-laughing. "How did you…? But you're called George, so it can't be you." My tail wagged as we gazed into each other's eyes. Then Isla tugged Dad's arm. "But that's just what Bandit used to do: stare until he got what he wanted."

Jake wriggled like he'd got fleas. "So, he's not actually my dog…not officially. He's a stray. I found him on the beach, and Mum made me take him to the kennels, but they can't track his owner so hopefully we can —"

"But he must belong to someone," cut in Dad. "And they'll be missing him." He sounded choky, so I whined and held up a paw. His eyes grew huge, and his breath trembled. "But Bandit's still with Mrs Mandeville."

Isla glared at him. "Phone her! Find out!"

I've had enough of this. I sprang into Isla's arms, and she lay on her back and cuddled me. Now she *had* to realise who I was.

For a wonderful moment, it was just us and the sky. Then Isla stood and shook her jacket.

I can do that! I did one of my best shakes, spraying sand everywhere. She laughed, and Jake laughed too, his voice jumping up then diving down again.

Dad was talking at the phone. He looked at Isla. "No answer."

"Try again."

"Hold on…hello?" He pressed the phone closer to his ear. "Who's this?... Oh, yes, you're Maud's friend… *She's what?*" His voice shot up. "Is she ok?" More short sharp words like rain jumping on Croaky's glass roof. "*When?* Why didn't you tell us? We would've been out looking for him, *anything* could've happened…"

He stuck the phone in his pocket, and my tail swished sand at his legs, but he didn't look at me. "Young man…"

"Jake."

Dad nodded. "Jake. I'm going to ring the kennels. If you could meet us there, perhaps we could clear this up? I've just heard that our dog ran away, and this little guy is *so* like him."

"BECAUSE HE IS BANDIT!" shouted Isla.

Jake's feet shuffled and he picked up my lead. "I'll phone my mum. She's having coffee in the cafe."

"*YES!*" shouted Isla. Then her nose wrinkled. "But Mum said to come straight home because she's making a special roast dinner for Grandad."

Dad's jaw tightened. "That's the first I've heard of it. I thought he'd cleared off after he left that note."

A wave of sadness swirled around Isla. "I haven't

seen Grandad for years, except for video chats."

"Don't get your hopes up." Dad pointed at me. "And don't get your hopes up about this dog. He might not be ours."

Isla put her arms around my neck. "I *know* he is!"

39. The Database Disaster

Why am I back here? I wasn't the only one who was surprised: The Keeper was staring at Hair-Horns. "I thought this young man and his mum were fostering the spaniel all weekend?"

She nodded. "Yes, they were but…"

Isla smiled. "George isn't George; he's *Bandit!* He went to live with this old woman, but she tried to steal him from us. And then he ran off, and I don't blame him. She was so mean." Isla's smooth forehead creased in waves, then she whipped out her phone and swiped it with her finger. "Look, that's Bandit, when he was nine months old, just before she stole him."

Dad wriggled like he had fleas up his back. "Mrs Mandeville technically *fostered* him for a year."

The Keeper's eyebrows shot up. "Run that past me again…"

"George might be their lost dog," said Jake slowly.

His gaze flicked from Isla to The Keeper and back to Isla again.

Isla arched her head, and pointed at The Keeper. "HE IS! HE'S BANDIT! I KNOW HE IS!"

"Isla, calm down," said Dad. "You're being rude."

Isla was full of pain. And love. I whined and brushed against her. It felt so natural, her hand stroking me.

The Keeper lifted a dark eyebrow. *"You just know?"* My hackles rose; I didn't like his tone of voice when he spoke to Isla. Then the Keeper said something to Hair-Horns.

She held out her hands. "I've checked the mobile number on the database many times, but I've always drawn a blank, and there's no landline at that address anymore. I'm afraid the owner can't have updated their details." She turned to Dad. "If you'd like to look at our other residents, sir…"

"But he's *our* dog!" Isla's pain dived inside me, making me whimper. Isla was unhappy, and that made me unhappy. I nosed her arm, getting even closer.

"What an *idiot*!" Dad's loud voice alerted me. He was facing the sky, arms outstretched. The Keeper spread his legs and arched his neck like he was Top Dog. I started to growl. Then Dad tapped his forehead. "No, *I'm* the idiot! I must've forgotten to update our address when we moved to the cottage — *and* I've got a new mobile number."

Isla gasped. "So it's all *your* fault if we can't get Bandit back."

The Keeper looked at Dad. "So, what was your previous address?"

Dad said something, and The Keeper glanced at Hair-Horns. She opened her mouth, but before she could say a word, Jake stepped forward and tugged The Keeper's arm. "But I *know* Bandit is Isla's dog."

"And how is that, lad?"

"Because he **LOVES** her."

Something important was going on; my senses were on high alert. Isla smiled at Jake, and her eyes leaked down her hoodie.

Then Hair-Horns was pointing to her file and smiling so wide that I could see all her top teeth. And The Keeper was shaking Dad's hand. And Dad's cheeks sucked in then his breath oozed out slowly like he was blowing up a balloon. And Isla was hugging me like she'd never let me go.

I hadn't a clue what was going on, but Blaze must have heard the commotion because she raced towards us. "What's up? Have you been chosen? Which one is it: the girl or the boy?"

Behind her limped Nero, his ears pricked in excitement. Something big was sweeping into me too. Then we were all wagging our tails like they couldn't stop.

Hair-Horns shook her head. "If I didn't know better, I would have thought these three had hatched some kind of plan."

40. Forever Family

The top half of the door was open, and a delicious smell was gushing out. Not just roast chicken, but the scent of wooden floors and smelly socks. I ran around the cottage wagging my tail and sniffing everything. The jackets on the coat stand. The soft slippers. The dirty trainers in the hall. It was like I'd never been away. I bounded into the kitchen, then my fur bristled and rose like a shield. Someone was sitting in the corner of the room. *Newspaper Man!*

"You've got it right there, Bandit," said Dad, who'd followed me in. His eyes narrowed, and his mouth was a straight line.

Isla joined us and skipped over to Newspaper Man. "Hi Grandad."

"My, you've grown, poppet. You can't tell people's height just from video chats." Newspaper Man's skin crinkled around his eyes as he spoke.

"What do you expect?" snapped Dad. "She was in

nappies last time you saw her."

"Whose fault's that?"

Isla wriggled and turned away. "Come on Bandit. If they're going to fight, let's go and explore. I can't believe you're home!"

I followed her into the other room where a boy was watching TV. He smelt like Harry, but he was larger. He didn't look up until I nosed under the crook of his arm. Then his eyes glowed, and he buried his face in my fur. "Bandit!" I licked his face, then as suddenly as he'd dived to cuddle me, Harry shifted and stared at the TV again.

"You love him, too. I know you do," teased Isla. Then she sucked in a sudden breath and tensed. She put her finger to her mouth and crept to the door. I followed. Dad and Newspaper Man were facing each other like angry dogs pawing the ground.

Dad fiddled with his ring, then he sucked in a deep breath. "Mum loved this time of year, didn't she?"

The words caused Newspaper Man to shrink, his back bowed over. "Yes, and she would have wanted the family to be together."

"So why was I sent away when Mum got ill?" The

ring was twirling so fast, it would ping off Dad's finger in a minute. Isla crouched beside me, holding me tight. Her trembles made me tremble too, as we watched Dad and Newspaper Man.

I heard a deep shuddering sigh. "She wanted to spare you the pain of seeing her suffer. She deteriorated so fast."

As Newspaper Man spoke, waves of pain swirled into me. He was sad, and he needed a cuddle, but Dad was standing straight as a stick, ignoring the outstretched hand. "It was far worse *not* seeing her. Why couldn't you understand that? Why couldn't I have stayed at home?"

"Son, it was killing me too. I'd pleaded with Mum, but she was thinking of your future. She wanted you to focus on your exams."

The room was darker, full of rumbling tension. I wanted to nuzzle up to Newspaper Man and comfort him by lifting a paw, but the angry heat coming from Dad made me hesitate.

"I failed anyway. How could I concentrate when Mum was in hospital?"

Newspaper Man reached out to touch Dad's shoulder, but Dad flinched like he'd been stung. "You should've told me the truth. You just said she was having some treatment. Why didn't you tell me she was dying?"

There was a creak as Newspaper Man sank into a chair. "I *did*. Remember it all happened so quickly... Maud was driving you over when..."

"I never said goodbye." The pain in Dad's voice dived inside me and made me whimper.

Isla sat down, her legs either side of me, and wrapped her arms around my neck.

Footsteps. Mum and Harry were here, and everyone was looking at Dad.

Newspaper Man clasped three fingers in his fist and twisted his wrist back and forward like he was wringing out a dishcloth. "She asked for you. The last thing she said was *I love you and Joe more than life itself*. It was tearing me apart that you weren't there."

The floor shook as Dad paced back and forward. "It's too late to tell me that now. I was stuck with Maud, then you made me go back there after your accident."

Isla let go of me. "Is that when you broke your back, Grandad?"

As Newspaper Man looked up, his voice grew softer. "I was bound up in my own grief — that's why I was mending the roof. I had to keep busy to stop myself from falling apart."

The feet stopped pacing. Dad's back curved, and I heard a choking noise. "But I swore at you when you were up the ladder, it was all my fault you fell…"

Newspaper Man pressed his hands on his knees and stood up. "That's in the past now, son."

The heaviness lifted, and the room felt lighter, although Dad's eyes were leaking down his face. "If only we'd spoken about it. I felt so bad—"

Newspaper Man nodded. "So did I, son. I knew you were grieving, too, but I didn't know how to reach you. You shut yourself in your room for months and hardly said a word."

"I know." The voice was a whisper. "I'm so sorry."

Isla tiptoed across and hugged Dad. Mum brushed past me, holding Harry's hand. She approached Newspaper Man, and they clung to each other.

I lay down, my head between my paws and kept watch. It felt like a moment for humans, not dogs.

41. A Surprising Gift

I'd been back in the cottage a month, and I was loving it. Dry dog biscuits and the occasional tin of sardines wasn't a three-course-dinner, but if that was the price for being with my family, it was nothing — well, not *quite* nothing, I'd do anything for a beef bourguignon or something **Licky-Platey-Yum-Yum**, but you know what I mean.

We'd been on lots of walks, and this was a trip in the car. I sat on Isla's lap, but she kept twisting and her anxiety got inside me, tumbling in my tummy like waves crashing against the rocks.

Don't leave me again!

"Bandit doesn't want to go either; he's whining," said Isla. "It's not fair! You didn't make Harry go, so why do *I* have to see her? She *stole* him!"

Mum sighed. "Look, if Dad's talking to Grandad again..."

Isla's body tensed. *"At last!"*

"Well, I think Grandad getting a dog was a good

idea. Now they can go on walks together."

My ears pricked. **WALK! Are we going for a walk on the beach?**

Isla relaxed, and her fingers combed my ears so they intertwined under my snout. "It's weird that Grandad's fostering a rottweiler. And one that's lost half an ear and he's all scabby."

"I think Grandad felt sorry for him."

"I guess." Isla's elbows were squishing me, but I didn't move; I wasn't going to lose her again.

Mum glanced over her shoulder. "If Dad can forgive Grandad, surely we can show a little kindness to a sick old woman, by visiting her. She might be lonely in the residential home."

Anger was pulsing through Isla's chest. She didn't speak, just glared at Mum.

"Well, do your best. We're nearly there." The car squealed, and the trees stopped flashing by. Mum looked behind her, then turned the wheel. "Jake found Bandit wandering on Rock Beach, right? Are you going to see Jake again?"

Isla wriggled then flung her hair back. "Stop going on about it, Mum, it's *so* embarrassing."

Isla was still in a mood when we reached a big building. Her feet dragged along the floor as Mum led us along a corridor with lots of doors. She knocked on one and pushed it open. I recognised the sticky spray that hung in the air. And cheesy feet. I hovered by the bed with one paw in the air, not knowing what to do. The cabinet was there and a picture on the wall. I was glad Croaky could still talk to that picture.

A thin hand reached out and patted the air. "Jasper, is that you?" Croaky's lips wobbled. "Fetch me a tissue, would you, dear?"

"He's not *Jasper*, he's Bandit!" Isla's voice was sharp. "And he's a *dog*!"

"Isla, remember what I said." Mum pulled the chair beside the bed.

"Prop me up a bit, would you?" Croaky flapped her hand, and Mum slid another pillow under her head.

"Ah, there you are, dear." Croaky patted me, then she pushed something over my eyes. "Maybe the bobble hat could be a little larger?"

I pawed the itchy thing off and Isla giggled.

"Now for your gift, young lady…" Croaky held out an envelope, but Isla stayed beside me and put her hands behind her back.

"Please; it would make me happy." Croaky flapped the envelope. "Jasper could do with some new clothes…" She leant over, and the bedding crackled. "And perhaps a little holiday for you all?"

"That's very kind of Mrs Mandeville, isn't it, Isla?" said Mum.

Isla looked at her trainers. "I s'pose we could give the money to Jake to buy a new dog; *He* found Bandit, not me."

I heard Croaky sniffing. "Well, whatever you think best…but Jasper has brought me so much joy, I just wanted to..." She looked down at me over her glasses. "You're not wearing a coat, dear?"

"He doesn't —" Isla began.

Mum waved her hand. "We left it in the car."

"Well, remember to put it on when you get outside, or you'll catch a chill."

Isla eyeballed Mum. "It's *baking* in here."

Croaky leant over and stroked my head. "I don't know where I would've been without my little Jasper."

Her voice broke into pieces.

I felt Isla tense, and she started to speak, but Mum elbowed her. "Well, it was lovely to see you."

"Oh, won't you wait for Celia? She's bringing a Victoria sponge."

SPONGE! I know that word.

We always had Sponge when Polly came over and our humans ate cake. Polly was my best friend and we had such fun. I'm glad her leg got better. Maybe one day I'll see her again and we can run on the beach together.

Croaky looked at me. "I thought we'd have a party, like *Friends Friday*."

"It's Tuesday," said Isla.

"Is it?" Croaky flapped her hands. "Anyway, we're celebrating."

Mum nodded. "And quite right: Bandit's safe and sound."

Croaky nodded. "'Ere, and did you know, they caught that nasty Mr Brown before he stole my life savings?"

"That sounds like quite a story," said Mum.

Croaky sat bolt upright. "You'll never believe what happened. We met at Jamaica Inn and then…"

Isla pulled my collar. "Can we go now?"

"Oh." Croaky's cheeks drooped, and her lips drooped in the V shape I recognised. "Remember your manners, Jasper. Open the door for the nice folk, and remember to turn out the lights; why do they never turn out the lights in here?"

42. Bandit's Favourite Place

The minute we arrived at the cottage, Isla whistled and waved my bandana. **Our Secret Code!** My legs tingled, and excitement fizzed down to my tail. I ran circles around her then stretched my front paws and bowed. She tied the bandana around my neck, and I knew where we were going. Exciting messages were flying in the wind. When we reached the sand, Isla put her arms around me, and I snuggled in, my favourite place.

Then, among the salty seaweed and seaside smells, I caught the scent of burgers and tomato sauce. And another scent I knew. I sat bolt up and the wind tickled my whiskers. A cry reached us. My ears pricked up. I scanned the beach, and Isla pressed a hand against her eyebrows. A figure ran towards us, hair flying in the breeze. Speeding past Jake was a sheepdog.

I barked a greeting. "Blaze, have you…?"

Blaze bounced at me. "Yes, I've been chosen." She

winked. "Race you to the sea!"

Jake ran after Blaze, then Isla caught him. Isla might be taller than I remembered, but she could still run like the wind. Blaze dashed back, but Isla and Jake kept running.

What do you do if Your Girl runs off with someone else? You snout around for a tasty tissue or a sweet wrapper. I may have lost my way a bit because of everything that's happened, but my nose is still a super detector. The world is still waiting and I need to explore.

Blaze and I nosed around the rockpools and strands of seaweed, then we raced into the waves. When we dashed back, Isla and Jake were standing close together. I dived between them and gave a good shake. One of my best.

Isla laughed and rubbed her face. "I should've brought that bobble hat Mrs Mandeville knitted for Bandit."

Jake's lips wobbled. "A bobble hat? *For a dog?*"

Isla ran her fingers through her hair and drops of water flew onto the sand. "Honestly, you have no idea."

"I think I do." Jake ruffled my head. "When we found Bandit, he wouldn't eat food unless he sat at the table, it was bizarre."

"That's weird. He's not that type of dog."

"Yes, but I guess he'd been with the old lady for…?"

"Too long." Isla sounded angry.

Jake nodded. "So perhaps he became like that to please her?"

Isla sat down and stroked me under my chin. "I still can't believe he's really home, I missed him so much."

I arched my neck and waves of joy washed through me. **Don't stop! This is what I love best!**

A soft sigh tickled my whiskers. "And I know he missed me. Dogs pine for their owners, don't they?"

"But for how long? How do we know?"

Isla put her arms around me. "Well, *you* did, didn't you, Bandit? And now you're back with us, you are never wearing clothes again. Only your bandana."

Jake laughed. "Oh yeah? Sure you won't send him to a pet salon? Get his nails done. I hear bright pink looks good on dogs!"

"No way, Bandit only gets washed in the sea." Isla rubbed my fur. "See!" She jumped up and edged towards Jake. Her hands were dripping with salty sea water, and she was holding them out to him like she was stalking her prey.

"Oh no you don't!" He leant back, but she was quicker. Now his cheeks were glistening, and he smelt salty.

I don't understand humans, they do the strangest things. They start fighting and end up laughing. Then they hug like they're one person.

When they broke apart, Isla flopped down on the sand and looked at the sky.

I remember this! I rolled over and kicked the air. Right, left, right, left! **This is so much FUN!**

"Hey, can I join in?" said Jake.

Isla laughed, then leant on her elbows and put her arms around my neck.

I nestled into her soft embrace.

I'm home.

My Thanks To:

All the wonderful people involved in TEAM BANDIT!

My lovely beta readers for your amazing feedback: Cathy Mee, Elisabeth Pike, Dawn Shearsmith, Bethan Auyeung and Lisa Allen.

Thanks to my brilliant eagle-eyed child readers: Raphael, Ruth, Joshua, Hannah and Holly.

It's so good to bounce ideas off other creatives and receive encouragement and helpful advice. Many thanks to the fabulous Funny Business critique group, and a special shout-out to Philip Kavvadias, a founder member, for your wisdom and sense of fun. And many thanks to my supportive local writing community.

Thanks to WriteMentor, the brilliant organisation that gives so many opportunities to progress in writing, and to Stuart White, its inspiring founder. I was thrilled when Bandit's Great Escape was listed as a Reader's Favourite in the Novel-in-Development Award 2023.

I am very grateful to Peter Thurman for the beautiful drawing of Jessie that I treasure.

I am blessed to have had two editors who have looked at different stages of the book. Many thanks to the wonderful Emma Read and Tasha Harrison for all your insightful edits and expert editorial advice, and for loving the character of Bandit.

A big thank you to Matthew and Rosie Jackson for all your hard work: Rosie, for creating the beautiful, fun illustrations that make me smile, and Matthew, for designing the stunning cover!

And finally, my love and thanks to my family for all your support, encouragement and computer advice. Especially to my husband Stuart for your amazing patience and fabulous work in formatting the book.

Dear Reader,
This is a story about a girl and her dog, about the pain of separation and the power of love.

Do you like writing, too? Here are a few tips that have helped me. Think of an interesting character, a strong idea, or an amazing place and weave a story around it. And humour always helps! Interesting and fun names are also a good idea.

Which CHARACTERS are your favourites in Bandit's Great Escape? Do you like their descriptions, how they speak or act, or all of these?

As I love dogs, I chose to write this story from a dog's point of view. We had a black labrador puppy when I was young and she was my world. I used my memories and strong emotions to create the character of Isla.

Bandit was inspired by my golden retriever. Jessie brought such joy, always welcoming us with a waggy tail and as many stuffed toys as she could fit in her mouth! And she always listened, whether you were happy or sad. She'd push her head under my elbow if I was reading and gaze into my eyes, asking me to stroke her. And of course, she always got what she wanted! Very sadly, Jessie passed on last year, but her funny mannerisms, her faithfulness and love live on in the character of Bandit.

Do you, or your friend or relative, have a pet? Next time you see the pet, imagine what they are thinking and why they react as they do. A dog's sense of smell is far better than ours, for instance, whereas our eyesight is probably better than theirs - unless you have a pet eagle!

Bandit loves food. He even says it's his hobby! What are your fun ways of describing yummy food? Which of Bandit's foodie phrases is your favourite?

1. Great Gulpy Guzzle!
2. Licky-Platey-Yum-Yum!
3. Gobble-Amazing!
4. Yumitty-Scrumitty!
5. Gobble-Gooey-Gorgeous!
6. Scrumlicious!
7. Whisker-Tingling, Drool-Dribbling-Good!
8. Licky-Likey-Scrum-Doodle!
9. Tingle-Tongue-Tasty!
10. Gobble-icious!

Which parts of the PLOT do you like best and why? Are there any parts that you thought would end in a different way and twists that surprised you?

When you're writing, try to put emotion and heart into a story and include problems that the main character has to face. I put Bandit in lots of tough situations he had to overcome at Croaky's house and in his quest to find Isla.

Can you visualise the PLACE where Bandit's Great Escape is set? I chose North Cornwall because I worked in Port Isaac one summer (before Doc Martin was filmed there), and I often walked through Squeezy Belly Alley - yes it really is called that! I loved exploring the beaches and walking in Bodmin Moor. Recently, I've visited Jamaica Inn and walked along the lovely Camel Trail. When I saw cyclists with dog trailers, I decided Bandit would sneak a ride in one in the story!

Drawings from Joshua Tabor (12)

Also by Rachel Rivers Porter

'Kiss of the Tsunami' is definitely worth a read – a gripping story about survival and sacrifice."
~ **Penguin Random House Writers' Academy**

Long-listed ~ **The Times / Chicken House Children's Fiction Competition.** 'A unique and accomplished novel with excellent, moving writing.'
~ **Reader's Report**

'I absolutely loved this book! As an English teacher, we will be looking to buy a set of these as a class reader. Beautifully written and deals with a variety of themes such as survival, hope and healing.'
~ **Jane Rayson**

'A heart-rending story with a serious message. Rachel Rivers Porter is an exciting, original new writer.'
~ **Bea Davenport – writer, lecturer, journalist**

'I was so captured by the story paralleling two young people and their mirrored experiences and the incredible descriptions of the tsunami and its aftermath. Some novels really do transcend age – this is one of them.'
~ **Miss R. Feasey – author of Jumpstart! Science**

RACHEL RIVERS PORTER was born in Hertfordshire where she spent much of her free time exploring her grandparents' garden and dreaming up stories. She studied at St Andrews University, then trained as a teacher.

Her love for animals has led to looking after injured birds, like the racing pigeon that crash-landed in her garden and inspired the adventure of hatching six ducklings in an incubator, and her young daughter having a Duckling Party that year! She has also looked after four chickens, three pheasants, tropical fish and best of all, her golden retriever. Bandit's Great Escape is Rachel's second book. Her debut novel, Kiss of the Tsunami, is for older readers.

Rachel enjoys giving author talks in schools and leading creative writing workshops. She would love to read your review of Bandit's Great Escape on Amazon and social media.

facebook.com/rachelriversporter
X: @RiversPorter
Instagram: rachelriversporter